WHAT THE **BIBLE** TEACHES ABOUT

HEAVEN

WHAT THE **BIBLE** TEACHES ABOUT

HEAVEN

Roger Ellsworth

EVANGELICAL PRESS

EVANGELICAL PRESS
Faverdale North, Darlington, DL3 0PH, England

e-mail: sales@evangelicalpress.org

Evangelical Press USA
P. O. Box 825, Webster, New York 14580, USA

e-mail: usa.sales@evangelicalpress.org

web: http://www.evangelicalpress.org

First published 2007

British Library Cataloguing in Publication Data available

ISBN-13   978-0-85234-662-4   ISBN 0-85234-662-X

Printed and bound in the United States of America.

The following pages are dedicated to my good friends,
Dennis and Jackie Miller

Acknowledgements

The following chapters were originally presented in sermon form to the Immanuel Baptist Church. My sincere and profound thanks go to these dear saints for eagerly joining me in the study of heaven.

I am also grateful to David Clark and Bob Dickie for allowing me to participate in the series *What the Bible teaches about...*, and for encouraging me along the way.

I especially appreciate my wife Sylvia, for dreaming with me about heaven. By the grace of our God, we will, dearest one, continue the journey there!

Contents

		Page
Introduction		9
1.	The one who has the right to speak about heaven	13
2.	Why should we be interested in what Jesus says about heaven?	23
3.	Heaven is a present reality	29
4.	Crossing the swelling tide	37
5.	The second coming of Jesus	45
6.	The new heaven and new earth	53
7.	A throne, a river and a tree	61
8.	The heaven of heaven	69
9.	The Father's house	79
10.	Jewels gathered	87
11.	Going and knowing	95
12.	Under heaven's spell	101
13.	Treasure in heaven	107
14.	Home before dark	115
Notes		121

Introduction

Reepicheep is one of my heroes.

Reepicheep is a mouse in C. S. Lewis' book, *Voyage of the Dawn Treader*. He boards a ship in search of lost countrymen and new adventures, but his mind is on a far greater adventure — getting to Aslan's land.

When he was but a youth, Reepicheep was told that he would journey to the Far East to find that for which he had always longed. This destiny was presented to him in the form of a poem:

Where sky and water meet,
Where the waves grow sweet,
Doubt not, Reepicheep,
To find all you seek,
There is the utter East.

After reciting the poem to his shipmates, Reepicheep says, 'I do not know what it means. But the spell of it has been on me all my life.'[1]

Aslan's land exists only in fiction, but Immanuel's land — heaven! — exists in reality! There Christians will find all for which they have sought and yearned. We were made for that land. It is home. The children's chorus says it so well:

This world is not my home,
I'm just passing through;
My treasures are laid up
Somewhere beyond the blue.

Yet we Christians are often wayward and easily lose our bearings. Before we realize what we are doing, we have dropped our eyes from heaven's glory to the fleeting things of this life. This world is our travelling place, but we are continually tempted to make it our stopping place. We are called to travel looking steadfastly forward to the glory, but, like little children, we take a few steps and then turn aside to examine some worthless little trinket or to fiddle with something that may be dangerous!

When an unbeliever sees a Christian fascinated with the very same things as unbelievers — the things of this world — he cannot help but conclude that Christianity does not offer much.

The pressing need of the hour is for Christians to be under the spell of Immanuel's land, just as Reepicheep was under the spell of Aslan's land. The confident hope of heaven will put a spring in our steps and a buoyancy in our spirits that cannot help but arrest those around us. And that same hope will lighten every burden and sweeten every affliction.

For a long time now, Christians have fretted about the possibility of being so heavenly-minded that they are of no earthly good. The truth is, the more heavenly-minded we are, the more earthly good we shall be.

So if someone asks me that old question: 'Are you a man or a mouse?', I hope I will respond by saying, 'It depends on the mouse! If it is Reepicheep, let me be a mouse. As he journeyed towards Aslan's land, let me journey towards Immanuel's land to find all that I seek. As the spell of Aslan's land was upon him, let the spell of Immanuel's land be on me.'

In *The Pilgrim's Progress*, John Bunyan writes of the pilgrim:

> So I saw in my dream that the man began to run. Now he had not run far from his own door, but his wife and children perceiving it, began to cry after him to return...; but the man put his fingers in his ears, and ran on, crying, 'Life! life! Eternal life!'[2]

May the pilgrim and his cry be true of us all!

1. The one who has the right to speak about heaven

Please read: John 3:13

We have often heard the words, 'If something sounds too good to be true, it probably is.'

Heaven sounds too good to be true. A place where there is no sorrow, pain or death! A place of perfect peace and joy! A place where there is no crime, no corruption and no parting! A place where there will be no policemen and no morticians! No prisons, hospitals, nursing homes or cemeteries!

But, unlike so many things that sound too good to be true, all of these details about heaven *are* true.

How can we be sure heaven is not just a pipe dream? When a great baseball player talks about his sport, we immediately accept what he says. Why? Because he is an accepted authority on the matter. He has instant credibility.

When a doctor speaks about medicine, we do not debate with him. Why? Because he is an authority on the matter.

But who can speak with authority on the matter of heaven? There is only one person in all of human history — Jesus!

Why should we consider Jesus an authority on heaven?

We have the answer from Jesus himself in the words of our text: 'No one has ascended to heaven but he who came down from heaven, that is, the Son of Man who is in heaven' (v. 13).

The Lord Jesus spoke these words to Nicodemus, who was a leader among the Jews. Nicodemus was intrigued by Jesus. He knew that he was not just another man. The things he had been doing proved beyond any shadow of doubt that Jesus had been sent by God (v. 2).

So Nicodemus came to talk to Jesus face to face. What did Jesus have to say about himself? How was he able to do all these things?

Jesus took Nicodemus by surprise. Nicodemus wanted to know if he came from God, but Jesus did not answer his question immediately. He began by telling Nicodemus that he must be born again. He must be spiritually born with a birth from above that only the Spirit of God can provide.

Jesus was telling Nicodemus that he could not possibly understand the things of God apart from receiving spiritual life from God. The natural man does not receive the things of the Spirit of God (1 Corinthians 2:14).

With that truth in place, Jesus assured Nicodemus that he, Jesus, had been sent by God. He had come down from heaven. This is not the only time that Jesus had made this claim. In

John 6:38, we find him saying, 'For I have come down from heaven, not to do my own will, but the will of him who sent me.' Other verses record similar statements from Jesus (John 6:32-33,51,58; 8:23).

Who is more of an authority on heaven than the one who has been there? We cannot send someone up to heaven to investigate and report on it. But Jesus has come down from heaven. He is the authority on it!

> Who is more of an authority on heaven than the one who has been there?

What are the evidences that Jesus came from heaven?

So how do we know Jesus came from heaven? I could claim to be an authority on nuclear science, but that would not make me one. Claims of authority must be substantiated. Authorities must have credentials!

What do we have here in Jesus? Is he someone who simply made an outlandish claim? Or is he someone who had the credentials to back up his claim?

Nicodemus came to Jesus because of the things that Jesus had been doing, and the things Nicodemus knew about were just the tip of the iceberg. We have far more evidence than Nicodemus! If Nicodemus was convinced, how much more should we be?

What is this evidence for Jesus? We will now look at six items of proof in support of his claim.

What the Bible teaches about heaven

The testimony of those who knew him best

The apostle John was called by Jesus to be one of his disciples, and John followed Jesus throughout his public ministry. For more than three years, John had a 'front-row seat' from which to see the life and ministry of Jesus. John himself described the nature of the association he and the other disciples had with Jesus, saying, '…we have seen with our eyes … and our hands have handled…' (1 John 1:1).

John wants us to know that his conclusions about Jesus were not based on a quick, casual glance. They came rather from a steady, intense gaze. And what had John concluded?

He sums it up in these words: 'And the Word became flesh and dwelt among us, and we beheld his glory, the glory as of the only begotten of the Father, full of grace and truth' (John 1:14).

John and the other disciples had studied Jesus closely, and as they studied him they saw flesh. Jesus was a real man! But they saw more than flesh! Shining through the veil of his humanity was glory; and that glory was nothing less than the glory of God himself.

It is important for us to note that John was not speaking about himself alone when he offered this assessment of Jesus. The other disciples had seen the same thing and supported John's conclusion.

Miracles

The miracles that Jesus performed also constitute incontrovertible evidence that he was from heaven. Jesus healed the sick, cast out demons, stilled storms, fed multitudes and raised the dead.

No mere man could do such things. The miracles were great in number, of all types and witnessed by many.

Supernatural knowledge

A third evidence that Jesus came from heaven is found in the supernatural knowledge that he manifested. He told people things about themselves that they had not revealed to him (John 1:47-49; 4:16-19,28-29).

Fulfilled prophecies

In the fourth place, there are the prophecies that Jesus fulfilled. We must not underestimate the significance of this. We are not talking here about Jesus fulfilling one or two, or even a dozen, prophecies of the Old Testament. We are talking about hundreds of prophecies!

What are the odds of one man in history fulfilling so many prophecies? There can be only one explanation for Jesus doing this. He was from heaven!

Jesus' resurrection

To these things we can add the towering fact of Jesus' resurrection from the grave, which itself is one of the best attested events in all of history. The apostle Paul leaves no doubt about the significance of Jesus' resurrection. He says that it 'declared' Jesus 'to be the Son of God with power' (Romans 1:4).

Jesus' ascension

Forty days after rising from the grave, Jesus ascended to heaven. The book of Acts describes it in this way: 'Now when he had spoken these things, while they watched, he was taken up, and a cloud received him out of their sight' (Acts 1:9).

The account also tells us that as the disciples stood gazing into heaven, 'two men stood by them in white apparel' (v. 10). These 'men', obviously angels, affirmed that Jesus had not only been 'taken up … into heaven' (v. 11), but that he would also eventually come again (v. 11).

Jesus himself mentioned his ascension at the end of what is known as the 'bread of life' discourse (John 6:32-58). Throughout that speech, he claimed to be the bread of God who had come down from heaven to give life to the world (John 6:32-33,38,51,58).

The clinching proof that he came down from heaven would be supplied when he went back to heaven!

When his hearers objected to his teaching, Jesus asked: 'What then if you should see the Son of Man ascend where he was before?' (John 6:62). Essentially, he was telling them to 'stay tuned'. The clinching proof that he came down from heaven would be supplied when he went back to heaven!

Each of these evidences is very persuasive and convincing, but we must understand that they do not come alone but together! How convincing they are as a package!

In light of these evidences, we should be ready and willing to listen to anything the Lord Jesus has to say on any subject — including heaven!

That brings us to yet another question.

Where do we find the teaching of Jesus on heaven?

Jesus' public ministry

Jesus himself frequently mentioned heaven in his public ministry. He spoke of rewards in heaven (Matthew 5:12). He told his disciples to glorify their Father in heaven (Matthew 5:16), and he taught them to pray: 'Our Father in heaven...' (Matthew 6:9).

He also urged them to lay up 'treasures in heaven' (Matthew 6:20). He spoke of angels in heaven (Matthew 22:30) and the names of his people being written in heaven (Luke 10:20). He also spoke of joy in heaven over one sinner repenting (Luke 15:7).

Heaven was obviously much on his mind and on his lips. Alexander Maclaren declares: 'There is a singular tone about all our Lord's references to the future — a tone of decisiveness; not as if He were speaking, as a man might do, that which he had thought out, or which had come to him, but as if He was speaking of what he had Himself beheld.'[1]

Matthew Henry adds: '...the truths of Christ are of undoubted certainty. We have all the reasons in the world to be assured that the sayings of Christ are *faithful sayings*, and such as we may venture our souls upon; for he is not only

19

a *credible* witness, who would not go about to deceive us, but a *competent* witness, who could not himself be deceived' (italics are his).[2]

But we must not limit his teaching on the subject to his own public ministry.

The Bible

We must understand that Jesus speaks about heaven throughout the entire Bible. The Bible was written by men who were inspired by the Holy Spirit, and the Holy Spirit is the gift of the risen Christ to his people (John 14:26; 15:26; 16:13-15).

Now we really have something to talk about! The Holy Spirit-inspired Bible mentions heaven 559 times.[3] And all of these 'instances' constitute the teaching of the Lord Jesus, who is the authority on heaven!

As we survey the Bible, we find that the Old Testament saints believed in heaven (2 Kings 2:1,11; Psalm 23:6; 73:24-25; Hebrews 11:8-10,13-16). And the apostles whom Jesus himself chose as his own special representatives obviously believed in heaven (Colossians 1:5; Hebrews 10:34; 13:14; 1 Peter 1:4; 2 Peter 3:13).

One apostle, John, even received special visions of heaven from the Lord Jesus and, on the basis of those visions, gives us more information about heaven than anyone else. It is not surprising that the book of Revelation mentions heaven more than any other book.

We have, then, identified Jesus as the one who can speak with authority on heaven, why we should consider him the authority and where we can find his teaching. But it is not enough to know these things. We must not merely acknowledge Jesus as the authority on heaven. We must embrace his teachings. We must conduct our lives in accordance with them. Only then do we truly acknowledge the authority of Jesus.

My knowledge of that life is small,
The eye of faith is dim;
But 'tis enough that Christ knows all;
And I shall be with Him.

2. Why should we be interested in what Jesus says about heaven?

Please read: 1 Corinthians 15:22; Hebrews 9:27; 13:14

We have discovered that Jesus must be considered the world's foremost authority on heaven. The truth is that he is the only authority on the matter. No one else can legitimately claim to have come from heaven. But Jesus can and does make this claim, and he has supported and substantiated it with many convincing and persuasive proofs.

We have also established that the teaching of Jesus on the subject of heaven can be found in the Bible. All of the Bible can be called the teaching of Jesus, and everything that the Bible says about heaven must be considered the teaching of this one who came down from heaven — the Lord Jesus Christ.

With those things in place, we must now turn our attention to this question: why should we be interested in what Jesus has to say about heaven?

The answer is supplied by the following texts:

'...in Adam all die...' (1 Corinthians 15:22);
'...it is appointed for men to die once...' (Hebrews 9:27);
'...here we have no continuing city...' (Hebrews 13:14).

We must be interested in what the Lord Jesus has to say about heaven because we are a dying people. Martin Luther writes: 'Life is a constant and daily journey toward death. One after another dies, and the living must merely engage in the miserable business of carrying one another to the grave. All of us are traveling the same road together.'[1]

We are face to face, then, with this grim business of death, and this is the reason we should be interested in eternal issues such as heaven. We are a dying people!

I can imagine us not being interested in eternity if we should never have to face it, but we do have to face it! Beyond death stretches the boundless chasm of eternity! Yes, the Bible tells us about eternity, but there is also a voice inside each of us that whispers the same. We instinctively know that we are not creatures of this earthly realm and nothing more. We know that we were made for eternity and to eternity we must go!

We do well, then, to think seriously about this matter of death, which is, of course, the gateway to the awesome reality of eternity. What does the Bible teach us about death? We will consider three truths.

Death comes necessarily upon us

Why is this the case? Why must we die? The answer of the Bible is very plain — and very unpopular! We are all 'in Adam', and 'in Adam all die' (1 Corinthians 15:22).

This takes us back to the beginning of human history. Adam, the first man, was given a very clear commandment from God regarding the tree of the knowledge of good and evil. He was told that death would come to him if he disobeyed God by eating of that tree (Genesis 2:17).

> We are face to face, then, with this grim business of death... We are a dying people!

We know what happened! Adam ate, and death came upon him. Some are puzzled by the fact that Adam did not die physically the same day he disobeyed. God said 'in the day that you eat … you shall surely die' (2:17). But Adam lived to the ripe old age of 930! (5:5).

The problem is resolved when we understand the various forms of death: spiritual, physical and eternal. Adam *did* die the very day that he disobeyed God: he died spiritually. His sin alienated him from God and made him dead toward God.

Spiritual death is really the central death. Physical death, which is the separation of body and soul, is the result of spiritual death, and so is eternal death, which is the separation of body and soul from God for ever.

The thing we must realize is that Adam was not just an ordinary man. He was the representative of us all. We were all present in him, and when Adam sinned, the consequences of his sin came upon us all. This is the reason the apostle Paul says 'death spread to all men' (Romans 5:12). Adam's sin constituted us all sinners and made us the recipients of the consequences of sin.

To those who object to this teaching, there is a very obvious answer: Stop dying! If you believe that sin and its consequences did not come upon us through Adam, show the fallacy of it by not sinning and by not dying!

Death comes indiscriminately upon us

Job states this truth in these words:

> One dies in his full strength,
> Being wholly at ease and secure;
> His pails are full of milk,
> And the marrow of his bones is moist.
> Another man dies in the bitterness of his soul,
> Never having eaten with pleasure.
> They lie down alike in the dust,
> And worms cover them
>
> (Job 21:23-26).

The author of Psalm 89 writes:

> What man can live and not see death?
> Can he deliver his life from the power of the grave?
> (Psalm 89:48).

The author of Psalm 49 points out that death prevails over both the rich and the foolish (v. 10).

The wise man may seek to remove the sting of death by making it an object of research. The foolish seek to neutralize it by keeping up a constant round of laughter and entertainment. But death doesn't go away. Charles Spurgeon observes: 'Folly has no immunity from death. Off goes the jester's cap as well as the student's gown. Jollity cannot laugh off the dying hour; death who visits the university does not spare the tavern.'[2]

Here is the psalmist's conclusion:

Like sheep they are laid in the grave;
Death shall feed on them…
And their beauty shall be consumed in the grave, far from
their dwelling

(v. 14).

Death comes speedily upon us all

How the Bible emphasizes this repeatedly! Life in this world is like a flower that soon fades (Job 14:2; Psalm 103:15-16). It is like a shadow that soon disappears (Job 14:2; Psalm 144:4). It is like 'a vapour that appears for a little time and then vanishes away' (James 4:14). It is like a tent that is erected only to be soon taken down (2 Peter 1:13-14).

Job captured the swiftness of this life in this way:

'Now my days are swifter than a runner;
They flee away, they see no good.
They pass by like swift ships,
Like an eagle swooping on its prey'

(9:25-26).

27

◇◇◇◇◇◇◇◇◇◇◇◇◇◇◇◇◇◇◇◇◇◇

Day chases night and night chases day, and we will all soon be there — in eternity!

◇◇◇◇◇◇◇◇◇◇◇◇◇◇◇◇◇◇◇◇◇◇

But despite all the Bible has to say about the brevity of life, multitudes are charging forward as if it were not so. Life is uncertain and death is sure, but many are living as if life is certain and death is unsure.

People who are wrapped up in the things of this world have little interest in hearing about eternity, but day chases night and night chases day, and we will all soon be there — in eternity!

Then it will hit us with full force that those who lived for eternity were wise and those who lived for the fleeting things of this life were colossal fools.

The Lord Jesus, whom we have established as the authority on heaven, plainly says: 'Do not lay up for yourselves treasures on earth, where moth and rust destroy and where thieves break in and steal; but lay up for yourselves treasures in heaven, where neither moth nor rust destroys and where thieves do not break in and steal. For where your treasure is, there your heart will be also' (Matthew 6:19-21).

3. Heaven is a present reality

Please read: 2 Corinthians 5:1-8

When a Christian dies, we say he or she has gone to heaven, but as we read the last two chapters of the Bible, we get the distinct impression that heaven comes at the end of time. So which is it?

The answer from the Bible is 'both'. Heaven is both a present and a future reality. It is something that the people of God experience in one way when they die and in another way at the end of time.

My parents have died. My father died in 1985, and my mother in 1992. I do not hesitate for one moment to say that my parents are in heaven, but I also do not hesitate to say that they are not in heaven now in the same way that they will be at the end of time. In other words, there is a difference between what we shall call the 'intermediate' state and the 'final' state of believers. My parents are in the intermediate state, but they will eventually enter the final state.

As we now consider this intermediate state, we must be very clear on one thing in particular. We are talking only about this state for believers in the Lord Jesus Christ. Yes, there is an intermediate state for unbelievers as well, but it is nothing at all like that which believers experience. Jesus' parable of the rich man and Lazarus makes this point exceedingly plain (Luke 16:19-31). What, then, does the Bible tell us about the intermediate state for believers?

It applies only to the soul

We consist of body and soul (Matthew 6:25; 10:28; Luke 12:20; Acts 20:10) or body and spirit (Luke 8:55; 1 Corinthians 5:3; 7:34; James 2:26).

Some suggest that we consist of three parts: body, soul and spirit, but the Bible uses the words 'soul' and 'spirit' interchangeably (Luke 1:46-47). William Hendriksen observes: 'The conclusion, therefore, is this: When you are talking about man's invisible and immaterial element, you have a perfect right to call it either *soul* or *spirit*' (italics are his).[1]

> You are conscious that you are a thinking and feeling person who inhabits a body.

Are you not conscious that you are body and soul? You know that you are not just a body, that there is something within you that is animating your body. You are conscious that you are a thinking and feeling person who inhabits a body.

30

Physical death amounts to the separation of the soul and the body. The author of Ecclesiastes says:

Then the dust will return to the earth as it was,
And the spirit will return to God who gave it
(Ecclesiastes 12:7).

When this separation takes place for the Christian, the body is, generally speaking, placed in a grave, but the soul does not die with the body. The body goes into the grave, and the soul goes to be with God.

What scriptural basis do we have for this? I have already cited Jesus' parable of the rich man and Lazarus. Both men died, and Lazarus was 'carried by the angels to Abraham's bosom' (Luke 16:22).

Since Lazarus was a beggar, his body may very well have been burned in the city dump. But his soul was escorted into the presence of God in heaven.

The rich man experienced something quite different. His body was buried, but his soul went to hell (Luke 16:22-24).

We find the same teaching in the words of Jesus to one of the thieves who were crucified with him. To this repentant thief, Jesus spoke these words: 'Assuredly, I say to you, today you will be with me in paradise' (Luke 23:43).

It is obvious that Jesus was speaking about the man's soul. We know that Jesus' body was placed in a tomb after he died, but Jesus said the man would be with him in paradise, or heaven, that very day. The only way this promise could have been fulfilled is through the soul of the thief joining the soul of Jesus in heaven after they both had died.

31

The classic proof of this teaching comes from the apostle Paul in his second letter to the Corinthians. He mentions being 'at home in the body' and 'absent from the Lord', and longing to be 'absent from the body' and 'present with the Lord' (2 Corinthians 5:6,8).

His point is not difficult to understand. For him to be 'at home in the body' meant that his soul and body were together, and, therefore, his soul was not yet present with the Lord.

But the apostle was looking forward to that time in which his soul would be separated from his body and would go to be with the Lord. At that time his soul would be 'absent from the body' and 'present with the Lord'.

We could also cite Paul's statement to the Philippians that he had a desire to depart 'and be with Christ' (Philippians 1:23). It is plain that he was equating death with his soul going to be with the Lord.

Now we must not take this teaching about the soul to mean that physical death is the end for the body. No, not at all! There is a glorious future awaiting the bodies of believers, but we are at this point dealing only with the intermediate state.

All of this leads us to yet another of the Bible's teachings about the intermediate state.

It is a happy, but incomplete state

There is much mystery about what the souls of believers are experiencing in heaven. We would like to know all about it, but the Bible tells us all that we need to know. Those souls are at rest (Revelation 14:13) and are with the Lord Jesus (Philippians 1:23). What more do we need?

Yet, having said that, we must go on to say that the souls of the redeemed realize that they are not yet complete, and they look forward to that completion. The soul of the Christian is in a state of perfect peace while it awaits the resurrection of the body, but because it is not complete during that time, it can be said to be 'naked' (2 Corinthians 5:3). The Christian looks forward, then, to the completion of his redemption.

We have a tendency to think happiness and incompleteness constitute a contradiction. If the souls of believers are happy, they are complete! If they are incomplete, they are unhappy! But there is no contradiction. Think of it in terms of a man and woman who are engaged. They are happy, but they are not yet complete! And they look forward to that time when they are.

The apostle Paul, who was given so much insight into eternal things, writes to the Corinthians about three states: the present, the intermediate and the final.

The present state is one of groaning 'in this tent' (5:1,2,4). We know about the sufferings and hardships that we have to experience while we live in these bodies. Because of these sufferings and difficulties, Paul was looking forward to that day when he would be 'further clothed' (5:4), that day in which he would receive his new body.

The middle step between our present body and our future 'new' body

The soul of the Christian is in a state of perfect peace while it awaits the resurrection of the body.

is the state which we have been discussing, the intermediate state. That is the time in which Christians will be 'unclothed' (2 Corinthians 5:4). They will not have bodies. That is not a bad state. It is just not the final state, and Christians look forward to the final state.

Redemption will be not complete until the bodies of the saints are raised and rejoined to their souls. How can the saints of God not look forward to that and long for it?

It is right to say that Paul looked forward to his soul being present with God. But it is also right to say that he looked forward to this because it was the step before the final step, when his soul would be rejoined to his body in eternal glory.

However, while we wait for that final state, let us be thankful to the Lord God of grace who has provided both the intermediate and the final states: a heaven to which we go when we die and a heaven to which we go when we rise! How good God is! And all this goodness is channelled to us through Jesus.

The intermediate state is the one in which we are 'unclothed' (5:4); and the final state is the one in which we are 'further clothed' (5:4).

The apostle Paul expressed this in these words: 'For we know that if our earthly house, this tent, is destroyed, we have a building from God, a house not made with hands, eternal in the heavens. For in this we groan, earnestly desiring to be clothed with our habitation which is from heaven, if indeed, having been clothed, we shall not be found naked. For we who are in this tent groan, being burdened, not because we want to be unclothed, but further clothed, that mortality may be swallowed up by life' (5:1-4).

Geoffrey Wilson explains:

The burden under which Paul groans is not the mere fear of death, but the separation of the body from the soul by death. Because death is the unnatural disruption of man's being as created by God, he could never be satisfied with a gospel which only provided for the redemption of the soul. He longs for something far richer than the bodiless survival of the soul after death … he cannot regard his salvation as complete until he is clothed with the resurrection-body of glory.[2]

The Christian's real hope is not the immortality of the soul but the resurrection of the body. He is glad for the former, but he lives for the latter.

4. Crossing the swelling tide[1]

Please read: Isaiah 43:1-2

Death is the doorway through which God's people pass from this world into the presence of the Lord. It is the way by which they enter heaven as it is now. When they die, their souls go into the intermediate state.

It is important, then, for us to consider the matter of believers facing the awesome reality of death. The above verses of Scripture can help us.

The people of Judah were facing extremely harsh and trying times. Because of disobedience to God, they were destined to spend seventy years in captivity in Babylon. It was God's judgement upon them.

Yet even in his judgement, God does not forget to be kind to his people. In these verses, he gives them two reasons as to why they should not fear what was lying ahead of them.

Firstly, they were united to him in a relationship that was unbreakable. They belonged to him. He had redeemed them and had constituted them as his people (v. 1).

Secondly, he promised to be present with them as they faced the trials and hardships of the future (v. 2).

These were not small promises. The circumstances the people were facing in Babylon would be of such a severe nature that they could be likened to passing through a deep river or walking through a scorching fire (v. 2).

God's promise to be with his people in their trials in Babylon has been precious to all the people of God who have found themselves in severe trials of one kind or another. It is a general promise that can be applied to every situation of difficulty.

But this promise has also been understood by Christians in a particular way, that is, as a means of comfort regarding death.

The swelling tide

Death can indeed be likened to a great swelling river that threatens to completely overwhelm us and sweep us away. John Bunyan's pilgrim found it to be so: 'They then addressed themselves to the water; and entering, CHRISTIAN began to sink. And crying out to his good friend, HOPEFUL, he said, "I sink in deep waters, the billows go over my head; and all his waves go over me."'[2]

Jonah used this type of language when he was in the belly of the whale:

All your billows and your waves passed over me.

...

The waters surrounded me, even to my soul;

(Jonah 2:3,5).

Of course, Jonah was actually surrounded by a great flood of water, but there was an inward dimension to what he was experiencing as well. That's why he talks about the waters encompassing his soul. The waters around him threatened to take his life, and the thought of death was in and of itself a mighty tide that seemed to overwhelm him.

Hymn-writers have picked up on the imagery of death as the crossing of a great river and have employed it in their works. Fanny J. Crosby's hymn, 'My Saviour First of All', begins:

When my life-work is ended,
and I cross the swelling tide...

Death can also be likened to walking through fire. We associate fire with pain and anguish of the most extreme kind, and that makes it a fitting image for the pain and anguish we feel when we face death.

The comforting, protecting presence

However, just as the people of Judah found strong consolation and comfort in God's presence with them in Babylon, so we may find comfort regarding the hour of death in that same presence.

When David contemplated death's grim countenance, he was comforted by the presence of God:

> Yea, though I walk through the valley of the shadow of death,
> I will fear no evil;
> For you are with me;
> Your rod and your staff, they comfort me
>
> (Psalm 23:4).

Have you ever noticed the shift that takes place in this verse? Up to this point, David has been talking *about* God, but here he begins talking *to* God. He pictures death as entering a valley. This suggests easy travel, as opposed to climbing a mountain. As he enters this valley a shadow falls over him. While they may appear quite frightening, shadows have no power to harm in any way.

Suddenly he becomes aware of the fact that something else is there. It is the very same Lord who shepherded him all through life!

David had not seen him before this (1 Peter 1:8), but he sees him now, and he is able to discern that he is carrying a rod and staff. The shepherd's rod and staff were sources of great comfort to his sheep. These instruments could be used to round up the sheep and to ward off enemies. As he views them, David suddenly finds comfort flooding over his soul. As a child of God, he had dreadful enemies, sworn to destroy his soul, but the sight of that rod and staff brought home the realization that he was absolutely safe, that no evil power could touch him.

When they come to the valley of death, many Christians find themselves suddenly beset by the enemies of doubt and guilt. David would urge each of us to look for the Lord in the shadows. He is sufficient to drive away all the enemies that gather around us at the hour of death.

As we look further at the promise in Isaiah's prophecy, we discover that God not only promised to be with his people in the river and in the fire, but to keep the river and the fire from harming them in any way.

That is not exactly what we would like to hear from God. We would like God to say that he will arrange it so we do not have to go through the waters of trial and the fires of difficulty, and we would especially like him to tell us that we will not have to walk through that swelling tide, that scorching flame of death.

But God says to the overwhelming majority of his people (only those alive at the return of Christ being exempt): 'You must go through the chilly waters of death. You must brave its scorching coals. But death has no real power to harm you. Its waters will not overwhelm you, and its flame will not burn you.'

The apostle Paul says essentially the same thing in his first letter to the Corinthians. There he chides death:

'O death, where is your sting?'
(15:55).

The Christian must still face it, but it is for him a toothless monster. Its sting has been removed.

> The Christian must still face [death], but it is for him a toothless monster. Its sting has been removed.

An assuring reality

How do we know all this to be true? How do we know that God's promise to be with his people in all their times of trial and especially in the hour of death is reliable? How do we know his presence is sufficient to take the sting out of death?

Our God would answer that question in exactly the same words he spoke to the people of Judah:

> ...I have redeemed you;
> I have called you by your name;
> You are mine.

There is all the assurance we need. God has redeemed us from our sin at the cost of sending his own Son to endure his wrath on our sins. By virtue of Christ's redeeming work, God has established a personal, friendly, even intimate, relationship with us. He calls us by our names. By virtue of what Christ has done, God has purchased us as his own prized possession.

If God has gone to such lengths for us, why should we for a moment doubt that he will keep his promise to be present with us in the hour of death, and that his presence will be sufficient to render death quite harmless?

Safely home

Oh, by the way, CHRISTIAN made it safely through.

His friend HOPEFUL said to him: 'These troubles and distresses that you go through in these waters are no sign that

God has forsaken you; but are sent to try you, whether you will call to mind that which heretofore you have received of His goodness, and live upon Him in your distresses.'

CHRISTIAN mused on that for a while, and then cried: 'Oh, I see Him again! and He tells me, "When thou passest through the waters, I will be with thee; and through the rivers, they shall not overflow thee"' ... Thus they got over ... also they had left their mortal garments behind them in the river; for though they went in with them, they came out without them.[3]

5. The second coming of Jesus

Please read: 1 Thessalonians 4:13-18

We have determined from the Word of God that the souls of believers go to be with the Lord when those believers die. We can say, then, that departed believers are in heaven now. Heaven is a present reality. But we also know from Scripture that the heaven they are experiencing now is not the same as the heaven they will experience at the end of human history. That final state, which we can also call heaven, will actually consist of 'a new heaven and a new earth' (Revelation 21:1). Heaven is, therefore, both a present and a future reality.

At this point, we are concerned with getting from the one heaven to the other. We now have the souls of dead believers in heaven and their bodies in the grave. We know this is not the final disposition of things. So how is God going to get believers into heaven in its final form?

The answer is provided by the apostle Paul in the verses of our text. These verses are referring to the second coming of the Lord Jesus Christ.

We will now highlight five points.

The Lord Jesus is most certainly going to come again

The world has not seen the last of Jesus!

Jesus himself promised that he would come again. On the night before he was crucified, he said to his disciples: 'I go to prepare a place for you. And if I go and prepare a place for you, I will come again and receive you to myself; that where I am, there you may be also' (John 14:2-3).

Do you remember what happened when the Lord Jesus ascended to the Father in heaven? The book of Acts describes it: 'And while they looked steadfastly toward heaven as he went up, behold, two men stood by them in white apparel, who also said: "Men of Galilee, why do you stand gazing up into heaven? This same Jesus, who was taken up from you into heaven, will so come in like manner as you saw him go into heaven"' (Acts 1:10-11).

> The very fact that the Lord Jesus arose from the grave and ascended to the Father tells us all we need to know.

Many centuries have come and gone since these promises were given to the people of God, but we should have no doubt about their fulfilment. The very fact that the Lord Jesus arose from the grave and ascended to the Father tells us all we need to know. He was no mere man, but God in human flesh. And God has no trouble keeping his promises!

When the Lord comes, he will not come alone

The apostle Paul makes this very clear, saying: '...God will bring with him those who sleep in Jesus' (v. 14).

Now who are these that will come with Jesus? Paul says they are 'those who sleep in Jesus'. All are agreed that this is a reference to dead believers. In the Bible, death is often compared to a sleep (Daniel 12:2; Matthew 9:24; John 11:11; Acts 7:60; 1 Corinthians 15:18,51; 1 Thessalonians 4:13-15).

Now there are only two parts to dead believers — their bodies and their souls. We know that Jesus is not going to come with the bodies of dead believers. He is coming for those bodies, as verse 16 so explicitly affirms.

If Jesus is not coming with the bodies of dead believers, he must, then, be coming with their souls.

This brings us back to what we noticed previously. When a believer dies, his soul goes to be with the Lord. Paul tells us that death means the believer's soul is absent from the body and present with the Lord.

It is interesting that the Lord Jesus himself made this point. After quoting these words from God the Father: 'I am the God of Abraham, the God of Isaac, and the God of Jacob,' Jesus made this point: 'God is not the God of the dead, but of the living' (Matthew 22:32).

The point is this: although Abraham, Isaac and Jacob died, they are not dead. Their bodies have long since turned to dust, but these men are alive! Their souls are in the presence of the Lord God.

This is true of all believers who have died. Yes, their bodies are in their graves, but their souls live in the presence of God and will remain there until the day of his coming. On that day they will come also.

When Jesus comes, he will raise the bodies of dead believers

Listen to Paul: '...the Lord himself will descend from heaven with a shout, with the voice of an archangel, and with the trumpet of God. And the dead in Christ will rise first' (v. 16).

What is the purpose of the Lord Jesus in bringing the souls of believers with him? While our text does not explicitly say this, there can be no doubt at all about it. Those souls are going to come with Jesus so that they can be rejoined to their bodies.

We must be profoundly aware of this: when the Lord raises the bodies of dead believers, those same bodies will be dramatically changed. He is not going to raise those bodies to be what they were before they died. No, thanks be to God, the aches and pains, the deterioration and the weakness will all be gone for ever.

What, then, will those bodies be like? Paul provides the answer in his letter to the Philippians: 'For our citizenship is in heaven, from which we also eagerly wait for the Saviour, the Lord Jesus Christ, who will transform our lowly body that it may be conformed to his glorious body, according to the working by which he is able even to subdue all things to himself' (Philippians 3:20-21).

The sum and substance of it is that whatever is true of the resurrected body of Jesus will be true of all his people when they are raised!

When Jesus comes he will 'catch up' living believers

There will be believers on the earth when the Lord Jesus comes. Many would have us believe that Christianity has long since outlived any use it may have had and is destined to perish. Some argue that the more advanced and learned people become, the more Christianity is doomed.

This might be true if Christianity were the invention of men, but it is not. The church belongs to the Lord Jesus, and he has promised that the gates of hell will not prevail against it (Matthew 16:18).

What will the coming of Christ mean for those believers who are living when it occurs? Paul tells us: 'Then we who are alive and remain shall be caught up together with them in the clouds to meet the Lord in the air' (v. 17).

Those who are alive when Jesus comes will never experience physical death. They will never go through their souls being separated from their bodies. They will rather be caught up, souls and bodies, to meet the Lord. This 'catching

The church belongs to the Lord Jesus, and he has promised that the gates of hell will not prevail against it.

up' will mean that they will receive their new bodies in the blink of an eye.

When Jesus comes, there will be a glorious meeting in the air

Who can imagine the sheer exhilaration and joy of meeting there in the air those beloved Christian family members and friends who preceded us in death? But the greatest glory of that moment is that we will meet the Lord in the air (v. 17).

Face to face with Christ, my Saviour,
Face to face — what will it be,
When with rapture I behold Him,
Jesus Christ who died for me.

Face to face — oh, blissful moment!
Face to face — to see and know;
Face to face with my Redeemer,
Jesus Christ who loves me so.

(Mrs Frank A. Breck)

Paul has one more word to add about this happy throng in the air, and that is that it will never be dispersed again. When the Lord Jesus comes to gather his saints, it is not so he can spend a short time with them, but so that he can spend eternity with them. Paul says, 'And thus we shall always be with the Lord' (v. 17).

What a comfort Paul's teachings were to the Thessalonians! They were concerned about their loved ones who had died. Thinking that Jesus would return before any of their number died, the Thessalonians were worried when some passed away. Were their dead loved ones safe?

The apostle Paul tells them that they had no cause for worry. Their loved ones were safe. Their souls were with God, and their bodies would be raised from their graves.

All believers of all time are safe. The God who graciously saved them will make sure that none are lost. All his people will eventually inhabit that new earth.

6. The new heaven and new earth

Please read: Revelation 21:1-5

We are right to say, then, that dead believers are in heaven today, but they are not in heaven today in the same way that they will be in the future. They are now in what we know as 'the intermediate state'. As the name itself implies, their state is not final. That is still to come. We now turn our attention to that final state, which we can also call 'heaven'.

We must constantly keep in mind that the intermediate state pertains only to the souls of believers, but the final state will involve both their bodies and souls. The apostle John was given a vision of this final state of believers, and we find his description of it in Revelation 21 and 22.

It is quite surprising that so many Christians do not seem to realize that the final state will consist of 'a new heaven and a new earth' (Revelation 21:1). Many believers seem to have the idea that the final state features ghost-like figures floating around in the clouds and strumming harps.

Others seem to think that the heavenly city, as described by the apostle John, will exist up in the air somewhere! They seem to have jumped over the words 'a new earth'!

So let us be clear on this — the final state will consist of believers living in new bodies on a new earth. And that new earth will have one city — 'the holy city, New Jerusalem' (21:2).

Other Scriptures which assert that there will be a new earth include Isaiah 65:17-23; 66:22-23; and 2 Peter 3:13.

Why a new earth?

A new earth! Can it be? I suggest that the word 'redemption' demands it. We know that when Adam fell into sin, all creation fell with him. Have you ever wondered about this? Creation did not sin, Adam did! But all creation was affected. The birds did not sin, but they were affected. The trees and vegetation did not sin, but they were affected. The fish did not sin, but they were affected.

> Redemption is, of course, God's plan to put things back to where they were before sin entered.

Why did God allow Adam's sin to have such a dramatic and devastating effect on all creation? We must say that his purpose in doing so was to show the huge, incalculable seriousness of sin. It was so serious that God allowed it to have cosmic significance.

Redemption is, of course, God's plan to put things back to where they were before sin entered. Redemption will finally put all believers back to where Adam was before he sinned. But it goes farther than that. Redemption must also put creation back to where it was before Adam sinned. Anything less would be defeat for God and victory for sin!

So I do not hesitate to say that the new earth which God revealed to John will be this earth restored to its original beauty and glory. It will be this earth put back in the condition in which God originally made it.

But we can and must go even further. God's grace and mercy are such that he will not be content merely to put things back to where they were. The new earth will be even better than the first! On that new earth, we will realize the truth of Isaac Watts' words about the Lord Jesus:

Where He displays His healing power
Death and the curse are known no more.
In Him the tribes of Adam boast
More blessings than their father lost.

Some Christians seem to spend a great deal of time vexing themselves over issues that are very trivial. One of the questions that I have heard frequently over the years is this: Will heaven be boring?

Of course, the people who ask such a question are usually those who think heaven will have ghost-like figures floating around in the clouds. If that is indeed what heaven will be like, we may very well conclude that it will be boring.

But that is not heaven! And the way to answer the question of whether heaven is boring is to ask if we find life on this earth to be boring. Most people will say they do not. So if life on an imperfect earth is not boring, why should we for one moment think that life on a perfect earth will be?

There is also another way to respond to those who suggest that heaven will be boring. We must tell them to look at the description of it which John gives in Revelation 21 and 22. How could anyone ever be bored with such a glorious place?

What will the new heaven and new earth be like?

The apostle John first tells us that there will be 'no more sea' (21:1).

What does this mean? The sea is a well-known emblem for noise (Psalm 65:7), turbulence and unrest (Isaiah 57:20). Sometimes it is even used as a symbol for evil (Revelation 13:1). The fact that there will be no sea in heaven is the Lord's way of saying that all these things, so typical of life on this earth, will have ceased.

There will also be no tears in heaven because 'God will wipe away every tear from their eyes' (v. 4).

How many tears there are in this world! I wonder how many tears are shed in the course of a week. The reason there will be no tears in heaven is because the most prolific tear-producers — death, sorrow and pain — will have been removed (v. 4).

How many tears have been shed over death? But in heaven there will be no obituary column in the newspaper and no mortuaries or cemeteries.

Sorrow will also be gone for ever. How many tears it has produced! Broken dreams, broken health, broken homes! And our hearts break with sorrow, and we weep and weep. But there will be no sorrow in heaven! The banishment of sorrow will be so complete that this life's best-known emblem for it — night — will not exist (21:25; 22:5).

Pain and suffering will also be removed for ever. Just think about it! Nothing will hurt! No headaches, toothaches or stomach aches! No stiff joints! No cancer!

Life in this world is such that we may very well often find ourselves saying, 'Enough!' Whenever we feel this way, we should glory in those words 'no more' (vv. 1,4).

If we 'fast forward' into Revelation 22, we find yet another 'no more'. There shall be 'no more curse' (v. 3). That word 'curse' encompasses the reason for all the death, sorrow and pain. It takes us back to the very beginning of human history: to the Garden of Eden and Adam and Eve.

We know the story very well. God commanded Adam and Eve not to eat of the tree of the knowledge of good and evil (Genesis 2:17); but they disobeyed that command. Their disobedience brought God's curse (3:14-19), and we have been living under that curse ever since.

Hear it well! Sin is the cause of all our problems. Sin is the producer of death, sorrow and pain, which have, in turn, produced all our tears.

In addition to all these things, sin also brings a kind of blindness with it, so much so that it causes us to blame God for the very things that sin itself has produced!

God is not the source of our problems. Sin is! If we do not like all the death, sorrow and pain we see, the thing for us to do is to become angry with sin.

Sin will not be able to continue its nefarious work in heaven. It will be a world in which sin will not be allowed to enter, and those who inhabit it will be those who have been delivered from their sins by the saving work of the Lord Jesus Christ.

The ones who go to heaven are the ones who have received him. Those who are still in their sins will be banished. If sin is banished, they must be as well!

This raises a very important and vital question. How can we reconcile the banishment of sinners with the joy of heaven? To put it another way, how can we say there will be no sorrow in heaven when many of our loved ones will not be there? Will not the absence of those loved ones spoil heaven?

This is a difficult question, and we have to admit that we do not know as much as we desire. We must be careful about assuming that we will view everything then exactly as we do now.

When we finally enter heaven, it will be with new bodies and new understanding. Our understanding here is so limited! When we go to heaven, we will for the first time see truly and clearly! There may very well be sorrow as we see loved ones depart from the throne of God. After all, the Bible does not say that there will never be any tears shed in the presence of God, but rather that those tears will be wiped away (Revelation 21:4).

> When we finally enter heaven, it will be with new bodies and new understanding.

That initial sorrow will surely go away as the people of the Lord gaze upon their Lord. There in his presence, they will realize that he is Lord of all, and they will magnify both the grace with which he saved and the justice with which he judged. They are both parts of the same Lord! And their admiration of him and their love for him will be so great that every other consideration will melt away, and they will gladly say: 'He has done all things well.'

This much we do know: the most important business before us in this world is, then, to break with our sins and receive the Lord Jesus Christ as our Lord and Saviour; and having done so, do all we possibly can to point our loved ones to the saving knowledge of Christ.

7. A throne, a river and a tree

Please read: *Revelation 22:1-5*

We have been studying the teaching of the Bible on the matter of heaven. In this respect, we are all familiar with the chorus that says 'This world is not my home, I'm just passing through.' Every Christian knows that is true. But if this world is not our home, where is it?

The Bible gives a perfectly plain and wonderful answer. The final home of all believers will be this earth restored to its original beauty and glory; that is, the beauty and glory it had before sin entered. Redemption demands nothing less!

And this earth will feature the heavenly city that is described by the apostle John in Revelation 21.

This home will be most glorious indeed because of the things that will *not* be there and the things that *will* be there. What are some of the things that will not be there? There will be no more sea, no more tears, no more death, no more sorrow, no more pain. And all these things will be gone because there will be no more curse. All of these things are due to sin, and sin will have absolutely no place on that new earth (21:8,27).

But what about the things that *will* be there? Our text mentions three such things.

A throne will be there

When we hear the word 'throne', we immediately think of someone ruling. And the new heaven and new earth will have a ruler. The throne John saw was none other than the throne of God himself.

Our circumstances are often such that we find ourselves wondering if God really is in charge. At the end of time, the answer will be abundantly plain. There will be only one throne, and it will be the throne of almighty God.

This throne is the major theme of the book of Revelation. The apostle John penned the visions he received for Christian people who were facing great difficulties and encountering severe persecution. These Christians must have often wondered: 'Is God really in control?'

The book of Revelation is also the account of men hating the throne of God and seeking to overturn it. But now we come to the last chapter of Revelation and the final chapter of the Bible. The tides of time have washed up on the shore of eternity, and the throne of God stands! God has the victory! That is the theme of Revelation.

Yet this is also the throne of the Lamb. There is no difficulty here. The Lamb refers to the Lord Jesus Christ in a particular capacity, namely, as the Redeemer. The Lamb refers to the Lord Jesus as the sacrifice for sinners. The fact that John saw one throne, and it was both the throne of God and the Lamb, tells us that God the Father and God the Son are united on this plan of redemption!

> John saw one throne [which] tells us that God the Father and God the Son are united on this plan of redemption!

Now think about this — if the throne of God means that God triumphs, and that throne is also the throne of the Lamb, it means that the Lamb triumphs. And to say the Lamb wins is the same as saying that the cross of Christ triumphs!

Ours is a time in which the cross of Christ is despised, ridiculed, scorned and rejected. It is true in the world, and, tragically, true even in the professing church! The preaching in many so-called 'Bible-believing' churches gives no place to the cross of Christ. All such churches would do well to question the wisdom of ignoring the very truth that will be given supremacy at the end of time!

Now let us turn to the second thing that will be in heaven.

A river will be there

This river will have a name. It is called LIFE! This river will be there as a constant and visible reminder of the ETERNAL LIFE that the people of God have been granted. Furthermore, life will be as typical or characteristic of that world as death is of this world.

Nothing is more typical of this world than death. Animals die. Vegetation dies. We die. Death reigns in this world, and its reign is always present for everyone to see. But there will be no death in heaven. It is the place of life. The Lord Jesus affirmed that he had come so his people might have life and have it more abundantly (John 10:10). The new heaven and new earth will be the marvellous fulfilment of his words.

Let us inquire further into this river of life. We should note that John saw it coming from the throne of God and the Lamb. There can be no mistake about the meaning of this. Eternal life owes its origin to God and the Lamb.

We can go further. Eternal life has its origin in the love of God and the love of Christ. Brothers and sisters in Christ, we could never have this life if God had not loved us. But, wonder of wonders, he has loved us!

> The sovereign, holy God who is clothed in majesty and splendour has loved guilty, unworthy, undeserving sinners!

The words that God spoke to the people of Malachi's generation are the very same words that he speaks to his people today. He says: 'I have loved you' (Malachi 1:2). We will never appreciate this until we understand the gap between the 'I' and the 'you', that is, between God and ourselves. The sovereign, holy God who is clothed in majesty and splendour has loved guilty, unworthy, undeserving sinners!

Boy,
sexu

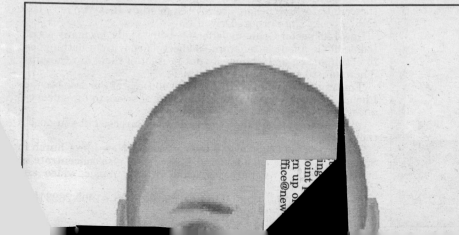

Finding a purpose

RELIGIOUS leaders in Durrington are hosting an event for local people to discover the purpose of life.

From Sunday, the New Life Church in Durrington is taking part in "40 Days of Purpose" with hundreds of other churches around the country, where people are invited to study Rick Warren's best selling book, The Purpose Driven Life.

New Life pastor Graham Jefferson said: "Sadly, for many people today, life is a four-letter word, 'a short journey from nothingness to nothingness', as Hemingway put it. A lot of them are thinking, 'There must be more to life than this!'.

"I'm tremendously excited about the 40 Days of Purpose because I believe that through it, people can find answers to life's deepest questions."

Anyone can participate in the 40 days of Purpose but you need copy of the book.

During the "40 Days" event, the services at New Life Ch Salvington Road, at 10.30am and 6.30pm, will also con explain life's key purposes using drama, mu Power presentations.

To s to obtain more information, call 0190 email life-church.org.uk

Out of that love, he sent the Lord Jesus Christ to this world, and out of that same love, the Lord Jesus went to the cross to die in the place of sinners. Don't you love the words the Lord Jesus spoke to his disciples on the night before he was crucified: 'As the Father loved me, I also have loved you...' (John 15:9).

How has the Father loved Christ? Without measure, without change and without end! And that is the way Christ loves us!

The apostle John further tells us that the water in the river of life is 'pure' and 'clear as crystal' (v. 1). That is a picture of God's love. It is pure and clear. Our love is always polluted or contaminated by something. But God's love is sincere and uncontaminated:

> Oh, love of God, how rich, how pure!
> How measureless and strong!
> It shall forever more endure,
> The saints' and angels' song.

That brings us to yet another thing that we will find when we get home.

A tree will be there

This tree is also called LIFE, and John tells us that it bears twelve fruits every month — not one kind one month and another kind another month, but twelve kinds each month!

What are we to make of this? It seems to me that the number twelve represents the people of God. So what God is revealing to John is that he will sustain all of his people throughout eternity! We often associate eating with fellowship. The fruit of this tree tells us that we will enjoy perfect fellowship with God for evermore.

The river, then, will always be there to remind us of what produced the life: God's love. And the tree will be there to remind us of the kind of life that love produced — one of perfect fellowship with God.

The tree of life carries particular meaning and significance for God's people. It takes us back to Adam and Eve in the book of Genesis. We remember that they enjoyed access to the tree of life (Genesis 2:9) until they fell into sin. And then that access was denied. Their sin caused God to drive them out of the Garden of Eden and caused him to station cherubim at the entrance of the garden 'to guard the way to the tree of life' (3:24).

What an incredibly sad picture! But here in Revelation 22, we find people being granted access to the tree of life again. How is it that these people now have this access? Let there be no doubt about this! It is only through the work of the Lord Jesus.

Let's go over it again! There is only one way for sinners to ever enter into heaven. Their sin must be taken out of the way. And there is only one way that sin can be taken out of the way — its penalty has to be paid. That penalty is nothing less than eternal separation from God.

Jesus came to this earth for the express purpose of dealing with sin. He went to the cross to receive its penalty. There on that cross he received an eternity's worth of separation from God for all who would believe in him. Now God only demanded that the penalty for sin be paid once. If Jesus paid it on my behalf, there is no penalty left for me to pay!

It is, then, through the work of Jesus that I, a guilty sinner, have access to heaven and the tree of life.

Now we are in position to see the theme of the Bible. It is PARADISE LOST THROUGH SIN AND REGAINED THROUGH CHRIST.

8. The heaven of heaven

Please read: Revelation 22:3-5

What will be the best part of heaven? Many would be quick to say that it will be seeing our loved ones. Others might say that it will be seeing the great heroes of the faith. Still others might choose some aspect of the heavenly city: the streets of gold, the river of life, the tree of life, the gates of pearl. With so many things from which to choose, I do not hesitate to say that the best part of heaven is stated in these words: 'They shall see his face...' (v. 4).

There is some debate about whether our text is referring to the face of God or the face of Christ. The difficulty is due to the previous verse mentioning 'the throne of God and of the Lamb' (v. 3).

To which person, then, was John referring when he wrote the words of our text: 'They shall see his face.' The answer is that we shall see both the Father and the Son. In the words of Don Fortner, this will be 'the very heaven of heaven'.[1]

◇◇◇◇◇◇◇◇◇◇◇◇◇◇◇◇◇◇◇◇◇◇◇
**Our first
sight of
the Lord Jesus
will be
thrilling beyond
compare.**
◇◇◇◇◇◇◇◇◇◇◇◇◇◇◇◇◇◇◇◇◇◇◇

Theologians have often called the sight of God 'the beatific vision'. The term comes from three Latin words that mean 'a happy-making sight'.[2]

I want us to focus on seeing the face of the Lord Jesus Christ. We shall first see him when he comes to take us unto himself (1 Thessalonians 4:17).

We may rest assured that our first sight of the Lord Jesus will be thrilling beyond compare. But the emphasis of the apostle John in our text is that we will go on seeing him through the ceaseless ages of eternity, and the thrill will never subside or fade. In heaven, we shall appreciate the words of David:

As for me, I will see your face in righteousness;
I shall be satisfied when I awake in your likeness
(Psalm 17:15).

Let's think about the thrilling nature of the sight of Christ.

Why will the sight of Christ be 'a happy-making sight'?

The face of Jesus will be a human face

What should we expect to see when we look at the face of Jesus in eternal glory? Yes, we should expect to see beauty and glory. As we look upon him, we might very well find ourselves calling to mind the words of Isaiah 33:17:

Your eyes will see the King in his beauty.

But when we look upon the Lord Jesus, we will see something which many seem not to expect — a human face! And as we gaze upon that human face, we will understand that we are there because of what we see there. It will thrill us because it will be a constant and visible reminder of what the Lord Jesus did to get us there.

Let me explain. We know that the second person of the Trinity came to this earth to take sin out of the way so that the people of God will be able to go to heaven. But what did this business of taking sin out of the way require of him? He had to take our humanity. He, the second person of the Trinity, added our humanity to his deity. He did not lay aside his deity. God cannot do that. He cannot cease to be God! But he added our humanity. So he was the God-man. Fully God, fully man!

Now we understand why it was necessary for him to do this. It was humanity that sinned, and it was humanity who had to pay the penalty for sin. Jesus could only pay for our sins, then, as a human being. He had to be one of us in order to do something for us!

Many seem to have a 'zip-on' view of Jesus' humanity. They think of him putting on our humanity, living in it for thirty or so years, dying on the cross and going back to heaven to resume being what he was before.

Those who hold this view fail to see that Jesus took our humanity for ever. When he arose, his body came out of that grave. In that resurrected body, he made several appearances to his disciples. In that same resurrected body, he ascended to the Father in heaven.

The Lord Jesus is in heaven today in our humanity, and he will be in that same humanity when we see him in glory. Have you ever wondered why it was necessary for Jesus to take our humanity for ever? Here is one answer: the fact that Jesus is in heaven now in our humanity serves as a guarantee that all of us who know him will eventually follow him.

As we look upon the face of Jesus, we will be reminded of God taking on our humanity for ever.

The face of Jesus will remind us of what he did in our humanity

We can go further. We will also be reminded of what Jesus did in that humanity. The first thing, of course, is that he lived in perfect obedience to the law of God. We must be righteous to stand in the presence of God and to see his face (Psalm 17:15; Hebrews 11:14). We do not have that righteousness, but Jesus provided the righteousness we need by living as he did.

The second thing Jesus did was to die on the cross. In that death, he received the penalty for sinners. He endured the wrath of God in their stead.

> As we look upon the face of Jesus, we will be reminded of God taking on our humanity for ever.

So it all comes down to this for believers in Christ: he took on *our* sins and we take on *his* righteousness (2 Corinthians 5:21).

As we stand in glory, gazing upon his face, we will surely be reminded of one aspect of his suffering in particular, namely, the battering of that face. Part of his suffering was to have his face so badly beaten that it was unrecognizable (Isaiah 52:14).

As we look upon that face in glory, our hearts will be flooded with gratitude as we realize that he endured that battering for us. By the way, in heaven we will also be able to see the pierced hands and feet of Jesus. Anne Ross Cousin writes:

The bride eyes not her garment,
But her dear bridegroom's face;
I will not gaze at glory,
But on my King of grace;
Not at the crown he giveth,
But on his piercèd hand:
The Lamb is all the glory
Of Immanuel's Land.

Matthew Bridges strikes the same note:

Crown Him the Lord of love;
Behold His hands and side,
Those wounds, yet visible above,
In beauty glorified:
All hail, Redeemer, hail!
For Thou hast died for me:
Thy praise and glory shall not fail
Throughout eternity.

(The Baptist Hymnal of 1956)

In *The Pilgrim's Progress*, John Bunyan has one of his characters, Mr Stand-Fast, saying at the river of death:

I see myself now at the end of my journey; my toilsome days are ended. I am going now to see that head that was crowned with thorns, and that face that was spit upon, for me.

I have formerly lived by hearsay, and faith, but now I go where I shall live by sight, and shall be with him, in whose company I delight myself.[3]

How should we respond now to what we will see then?

The happy-making sight of Christ in eternity should make us happy now.

Happy to be saved

We should be happy to be saved. As Moses prepared to take his leave of the children of Israel, he said:

> Happy are you, O Israel!
> Who is like you, a people saved by the LORD…
>
> (Deuteronomy 33:29).

Saved by the Lord! Those four words contain fabulous wealth. The word 'saved' implies danger. There can be no salvation if there is no danger. The people of God have been delivered from terrible danger indeed. The Bible leaves no doubt about this. It affirms that we are all sinners, and the penalty for our sins is nothing less than the eternal wrath of God (John 3:36; Romans 1:18; Ephesians 5:6; 2 Thessalonians 1:9).

The Bible further emphasizes that we are absolutely helpless to deliver ourselves from the wrath of God. Eternal salvation means that the Lord has done for his people that which they could not possibly do for themselves. When God's people finally come into his presence they will know very well what they should know now: that salvation is entirely the Lord's doing. Saved by the Lord! Charles Spurgeon writes:

> Why that one word 'saved' is enough to make the heart dance as long as life remains. 'Saved!' Let us hang out our banners and set the bells a-ringing. Saved! What a sweet sound it is to the man who is wrecked and sees the vessel going down, but at that moment discovers that the life-boat is near and will rescue him from the sinking ship. To be snatched from devouring fire, or saved from fierce disease, just when the turning point has come, and death appears imminent, these also are occasions for crying, 'Saved.' But to be rescued from sin and hell is a greater salvation still, and demands a louder joy. We will sing it in life and whisper it in death, and chant it throughout eternity — saved by the Lord.[4]

Spurgeon also says, '...I would fire your hearts with enthusiasm towards him who loved you before the earth was, who, having chosen you, purchased you with a price immense, brought you out from among the rest of mankind by his power, separated you unto himself to be his people for ever, and who loves you with a love that will never weary nor grow cold, but will bring you unto himself and seat you at his right hand for ever and ever.'[5]

Happy to obey

The Lord Jesus expects his people to obey his commands. The same penetrating question he put to his disciples applies to us: 'But why do you call me "Lord, Lord", and do not do the things which I say?' (Luke 6:46).

We know that the Lord is worthy of our obedience, and we even have within us the desire to obey. But we still struggle with it. We are always selective, obeying those commands that do not bind us too much, and partial in our obedience, obeying no command as fully as we ought.

Our struggle to obey stems from not realizing as much as we should how very much we owe. Tell me what the Lord has done for you, and I will tell you what you feel like doing for the Lord! The greater our understanding and appreciation of salvation is, the greater our desire to obey will be. Those who know salvation to be the eternal, sovereign God plucking them out of eternal ruin and bestowing upon them unspeakable privileges find that the commandments of God are not 'burdensome' (1 John 5:3).

Happy to worship

We know that our worship in heaven will exalt the triune God for the redeeming work of the Lord Jesus Christ (Revelation 5:9-14). Should not our worship now be doing the same?

The worship of heaven will serve as a rebuke to those 'trendy' folks who try to bring into worship here innovations that will appeal to people. In heaven, we will all finally see that which should have been apparent to us all along: worship is not about us but about the sovereign, majestic God who stooped to us in amazing grace.

Happy to serve

The people of God will serve him in heaven (Revelation 22:3). It will not be a place of idleness. We can rest assured that our service in heaven will be richly fulfilling. The dragging weight of sin will be gone, and the wonder of our salvation will so grip us that we will serve freely and gladly.

But the service of heaven, marvellous as it will be, can never replace service here. This life gives us a unique opportunity to work for our Lord, and that opportunity can never be repeated.

9. The Father's house

Please read: John 14:1-6

The final state of believers will be living on a new earth, which will feature the New Jerusalem (Revelation 21:1-2).

The Lord Jesus told his disciples about this final state during the night on which he spoke the verses above. He gave this final state a most wonderful name — the Father's house.

How do we know that Jesus had the final state in mind when he spoke these words? How do we know he was not speaking about the intermediate state? The answer is provided in verse 3: 'And if I go and prepare a place for you, I will come again and receive you to myself; that where I am, there you may be also.'

The souls of believers go into the intermediate state at the time of death. They will not be ushered into the final state until Jesus comes, and Jesus very clearly ties the Father's house to his coming (v. 3). He is, therefore, speaking here about the final state.

The occasion

It is the night before Jesus was to be crucified. He is with his disciples in an upper room in the city of Jerusalem. And he is on a mission of comfort. These men were crushed with sorrow because he has told them that he is about to leave them. He will soon die!

Jesus had often spoken of his death to these men, but on those occasions it all seemed so distant and unreal.

On this night it is all agonizingly real and inescapable. There is something very solemn and weighty about everything Jesus says and does on this night. The washing of their feet, the instituting of a supper by which they were to remember his death (Luke 22:14-20), the statements that one of them would betray him and another would deny him — all of these things give his death a strange immediacy.

Then what they had been feeling throughout the evening hours is clearly stated by the one whom they had come to love so much: he is going to leave them (John 13:36).

They are shattered by it all. How could they ever go on without him? What would now become of their dream that he would set up an earthly kingdom? These questions and more build up in their hearts and crash against their emotions with sledgehammer force.

I am very glad that the Lord Jesus responded to the troubled hearts of his disciples by speaking to them about his Father's house (v. 1). We live in a different world but we still feel the disciples' pain. Serious illness comes to a loved one or to us, and our hearts are troubled. Society creaks and groans under her massive load of sin, and our hearts are troubled. Loved ones die, and our hearts are troubled. We live in a day in which cancer racks our bodies, tension destroys families and financial hardship ruins our dreams. Ours is a day in which babies are casually discarded in hospital waste disposal units, crime ravages our streets, hunger stalks the poor, and immorality parades across our television screens. And, like the disciples, we sigh and wonder and ask questions. How can such things be? How can we face another day? What does the future hold?

Troubled hearts! We have to agree with the words of J. C. Ryle:

> Heart-trouble is the commonest thing in the world. No rank, or class, or condition is exempt from it. No bars, or bolts, or locks can keep it out.[1]

We sometimes get frustrated because we know the Lord has the power to remove our troubles, and yet he often refuses to do so. Instead, he usually does the very same thing with us that he did with those disciples. He calls us to look beyond the troubles of this life to that glorious place that awaits all the children of God.

The medicine Jesus gave those men that night is still good today. No matter what troubles us, thinking about the Father's house will help. His cure for their troubled hearts, then, was not to remove the trouble but to call them to look beyond it to something higher and better and nobler.

He calls us to look beyond the troubles of this life to that glorious place that awaits all the children of God.

The place of the Father

What can we say about heaven from this term the 'Father's house'?

Home

Heaven is the place where the Father is. So it is home. Much of what troubles our hearts in this life comes from our trying to make this world home. We easily fall into the trap of thinking this world is home, and if we cannot be here, heaven is the next best option. But the truth is, this world is not our home. We are strangers and pilgrims here. This world is a strange land to us.

Provision

If heaven is the Father's house, it is a place of plentiful provision. Our earthly fathers provide to the best of their abilities for our needs here; our heavenly Father, who has no lack of ability, will provide abundantly for us there.

Protection

If heaven is the Father's house, it is a place of unfailing protection. Fathers here try to protect their families. Oftentimes they are unable to do so. But the heavenly Father will unerringly protect us. Nothing will be able to touch us in heaven.

Pleasure

If heaven is the Father's house, it is a place of delight and pleasure. Many of us get most of our happiness in this life from our homes, but our homes here are often tainted with misunderstanding and conflict. That home will give us perfect delight for there will be no misunderstanding or conflict there.

The place of many mansions

The word 'mansions' implies lasting dwelling-places. In this life, we live in temporary houses that are subject to all kinds of catastrophes, and we move from one place to another. In heaven we shall finally be settled for ever.

How many mansions will there be in heaven? Enough for each child of God to have a place of his own! The greatest believers will be there, but, thank God, the feeblest saint of God will be there also. And all will be monuments to the grace of God that saved them.

Heaven is going to be wonderful! When a Christian dies, we sometimes talk as if it were a great calamity. His death may be very difficult for us, but it is certainly no calamity for him.

The preparation of the place

Jesus told the disciples that he was going to prepare a place for them. Some take those words to mean that Jesus is running around heaven with hammer, nails, boards and saws, building mansions. But the Christ who created the universe by merely speaking does not need to drive nails to build mansions.

Jesus was talking about what he would do the very next day on the cross. That is how he prepared a place for those disciples. By dying in their stead! By taking the penalty that their sins deserved!

Perhaps your response to all of this is to say: 'Yes, heaven sounds wonderful, but how can we know it's not just a pipe dream?' The answer is this: the very next day Jesus went to that cross! There he received the wrath of God in the place of sinners. If he was willing to go to that extent, we should not allow ourselves to doubt for one moment that he will go the rest of the way, that is, receiving his people into eternal glory. The hard work was done on the cross. The rest is easy!

The way to the place

It would not matter for a moment that heaven is the most glorious place imaginable if there were no way for us to get there. But there is a way! And Jesus left no room for doubt about the nature of that way. He is the way! He says: 'I am the way, the truth, and the life. No one comes to the Father except through me' (v. 6).

> Jesus is the way to heaven because he is both the truth and the life.

Although Jesus mentions three things — way, truth and life — it is the 'way' that predominates. I am suggesting that these three terms are not equivalent or coordinate. To put it another way, Jesus is the way to heaven because he is both the truth and the life. He is the way to heaven because he reveals the truth to us and because he grants life to us.

What is wrong with the sinner? The Bible says he is blind to his situation. He does not see that he needs a way out of his sin or a way into heaven.

The Bible also portrays sinners as being dead in their sins (Ephesians 2:1). They have no power in and of themselves to do anything about their sins. Dead people cannot see, but even if sinners could see the way to heaven, they could not walk in it.

Jesus becomes the way to heaven for sinners by doing two things. He opens their eyes to see the truth, causing them to see their own sinfulness and to see him as the Saviour. After causing them to see the way, the Lord Jesus gives them life. He quickens them so they can walk in the way.

Jesus is the way to the heaven of which he spoke by virtue of being the truth and the life. In other words, he is the way to heaven because he enlightens our minds to understand the truth and because he grants spiritual life to us.

10. Jewels gathered

Please read: Malachi 3:16-18

The theme of heaven is far greater than our ability to understand. Understanding how small and limited we are, the Lord graciously helps us, although he does not tell us everything we would like to know about the matter. Yet he does help us to understand something of the nature of heaven by allowing us to peer at it through one lens and then another.

The lens he gives us in the verses of our text is of God gathering his jewels. Think about it! Heaven will be the place of God's gathered jewels!

There is joy in the jewels

Who are God's jewels? They are his people. They are those who belong to him through faith in the redeeming work of his Son, Jesus Christ.

I ask you to believe this. I think I know how some of you feel about yourselves. Keenly conscious of your many sins, your coldness of heart and your little faith, you find it very hard to think of yourself as one of God's jewels. A jewel is something that has value. It is something that is highly prized. And you doubt that you have any value. You doubt that God could ever prize you.

If I were to ask you to select a word to describe how God feels about you, it would not be the word 'jewel'. You might choose the word 'trash', or the word 'rubbish', but you certainly would not choose the word 'jewel'.

I do not want for one minute to minimize our sinfulness or in any way make us feel good about our sins. But I want to affirm that God's grace is greater than our sins and that those sins cannot override, destroy or negate the grace of God.

God looks at his people differently than his people look at themselves. I have talked about looking at heaven through different lenses. Now I have to tell you that God looks at his people through the lens of Christ. It is through Christ and Christ alone that we are acceptable to God. And not just acceptable, but prized and treasured! Thank God for his different way of seeing things!

Do you remember that passage in Isaiah in which the Lord tells his people that the walls of Jerusalem are ever before him? (Isaiah 49:16). That is one remarkable passage! God addressed those words to the Jewish people when

> God's grace is greater than our sins and those sins cannot override, destroy or negate the grace of God.

they were in captivity in Babylon. At that time, there was no Jerusalem. The city had been destroyed by the Babylonians. And when those captives thought of Jerusalem, all they could see with the eyes of their minds was ruins. But God, with his different way of looking at things, saw walls!

Let me go further. As those people thought about the ruins of Jerusalem, they thought about their sins. Their sins caused those ruins! It was their disobedience to God that caused the Lord to bring the Babylonians in! The fact that God saw walls instead of ruins tells us both that he was not through with Jerusalem and that their sins, serious as they were, could not defeat God's purpose for them. The walls of Jerusalem could be demolished and ruined, but God's purpose for them could never be.

Alan Redpath writes:

> If someone feels in his heart the situation is hopeless, I say you are looking at the ruins of life, while God looks at the walls. You look at what you have been and you are conscious of awful failure, but bless the Lord, He sees you in Christ, as what He intends you to be. He sees you as what you long to be in your best moments. He sees you as what you will be when the grace of God has finished the task.[1]

I remind you that God looks at his people through the lens of Christ. I do not tell you that you are God's jewels so that you will have higher self-esteem, but so that you will more highly esteem Christ.

That now brings us to a second matter.

There is joy in the gathering

This passage tells us that a day is coming when God will 'make' his people his jewels. The word 'make' refers to God making everyone know that his people are his jewels. The promise, then, is of a day when God will make it clear that his people really do belong to him. God's people are not prized in this world, but they will be prized in the world to come.

The saints of Malachi's generation certainly needed this word. They were living in very difficult and trying times. It was a day of tremendous apathy toward spiritual things, a day in which people were merely going through the motions with hearts that were far from God.

It was also a day of scepticism and doubt. Wicked people were so flourishing and prospering that the righteous people were left wondering if there was any point to serving God.

Some of the people were so discouraged by this that they were actually saying: 'Everyone who does evil is good in the sight of the LORD, and he delights in them' (2:17). Another comment they were making was: 'So now we call the proud blessed, for those who do wickedness are raised up. They even tempt God and go free' (3:15).

The people of Malachi's time were not the only ones who struggled with this problem. The psalmist Asaph wrote a lengthy piece in which he wondered why the wicked prospered while the people of God suffered. At one point he says: 'Behold, these are the ungodly, who are always at ease; they increase in riches. Surely I have cleansed my heart in vain, and washed my hands in innocence. For all day long I have been plagued, and chastened every morning' (Psalm 73:12-14).

Asaph begins this psalm by confessing that he had allowed this problem to drive him to the very brink of despair. He says: '…my feet had almost stumbled; my steps had nearly slipped' (v. 2).

Almost every child of God can say the same problem has caused him to stumble or slip at one time or another. Most of us would have to admit that we, in the light of how blessed the wicked are, have wondered with Malachi's people if it is in fact vain to serve the Lord (3:14).

Even unbelievers themselves pick up on this problem. When Christians talk to them about the Lord Jesus Christ, they say: 'Look, I'm getting along just as well as you are. Why do I need Christ?'

The difference between believers and unbelievers may not always be apparent in this life, but, in the words of T. V. Moore, there is coming a 'great day of final adjustment ... in which all seeming anomalies of the present shall be fully explained and wholly removed forever'.[2]

In this world, the people of God are regarded as anything but precious jewels. In this world, they are scattered amidst the dirt and mire. They are often treated with disdain and disgust.

In heaven they will at long last be rewarded and vindicated. Nothing they have ever done for the Lord's honour and glory will be forgotten because God is keeping a 'book of remembrance' (3:16).

It was a common practice among ancient kings to keep such a book. Any subject who rendered a service to the king had his name and what he had done noted in that book, and in due time the king would reward him (Esther 6:1).

God is keeping such a book of remembrance that even the smallest act of service is noted. When the people of God get together and speak to one another about their God, their slightest whisper of praise is noted and will be rewarded.

The Lord Jesus struck this same note when Peter asked what he and the other disciples would receive for following him. Jesus said everyone who follows him 'shall receive a hundredfold' (Matthew 19:29).

The dawning of that glorious eternal day is going to be an occasion of unspeakable joy and praise. Malachi says it will be a day when God's people will 'skip about like calves from the stall' (4:2, New American Standard Bible).

With a God who regards us as his precious jewels and who rewards even our minutest form of service, why should we worry about the wicked prospering more than Christians in this life?

On that day, the debate about whether it is wise to serve God will cease for ever. To the people of Malachi's day, it often appeared that there was no point in being righteous. The line between the righteous and the wicked was so horribly blurred that it seemed as if one was as good as another. But eternity will bring clarity to all muddled situations, and it will be obvious that the righteous were wise.

Like the people of Malachi's generation, we sometimes envy the wicked, but no one will envy them in eternity. For them, the eternal day will be one of raging fire and they will be like stubble in the midst of it. The Lord says:

> We sometimes envy the wicked, but no one will envy them in eternity.

…And the day which is coming shall burn them up

(4:1).

Instead of envying the wicked, we should feel deep compassion and pity for them. The happiness they enjoy in this life is all the happiness they will receive. It is utter foolishness to envy anyone who is headed for eternal destruction (Psalm 73:17-20).

The people of God are called, then, not to look to this life as the source of their happiness, and they are not to expect God to finally vindicate them in this life. We get into trouble when we expect this life to yield the things that only eternity can yield.

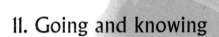

11. Going and knowing

Please read: 1 John 5:11-13

The glories of heaven are such that two questions ought to be pressing upon us more than any others: how can we go to heaven and how can we know we are going?

The apostle John covers both bases in the verses of our text.

How can we go to heaven?

The apostle emphatically tells us that there is only one way to heaven, and that way is Jesus Christ.

John tells us that eternal life is in God's Son (v. 11). He adds: 'He who has the Son has life; he who does not have the Son of God does not have life' (v. 12). Can words be plainer? If you have the Son of God, you have eternal life. If you do not have the Son of God, you do not have eternal life.

The question now is: How do we have the Son of God? How do we possess him? This same apostle gives the answer so very clearly in the Gospel he wrote (John 3:16; 3:36; 6:29, 40, 47). We possess Christ, then, by believing in him or by faith in him.

There is danger in that word 'believe'. The danger is that we will take it to mean mere intellectual assent. Many think they have true faith in Christ, but they have done nothing more than accept mere facts about Christ. They believe there was such a man. They believe that he was born in Bethlehem. They believe that he died on the cross. They even believe that he rose again.

But when the New Testament uses the word 'believe', it always carries with it the idea of commitment. I like to think of it in terms of marriage. Before my wife and I were married, I understood marriage, and I agreed with it! Was I married? No! I was not married until I committed myself to 'love and cherish' my wife until death.

It is not enough to know what the Bible says about Jesus. It is not enough even to believe that the Bible's account of Jesus is true. The question we must ask ourselves, then, is whether we have committed ourselves to the Lord Jesus Christ. Are we depending on him, and him alone, for a right standing with God and for acceptance into heaven?

More specifically, are we trusting in what he did in his life, his death and his resurrection for our eternal salvation? John uses the word 'propitiation' (4:10) in describing what the Lord Jesus did for sinners.

Going to heaven means trusting in the 'propitiation' of Christ. That word means 'to satisfy or appease wrath'. Here we are in our sins, and here God is in his holiness. God's holiness means he cannot be neutral or ambivalent about our sins. He must judge our sins.

> God's holiness means he cannot be neutral or ambivalent about our sins.

Now here is the wrath of God coming toward us, but Jesus steps in and provides propitiation. He appeases God's wrath. The only way for God's wrath to be appeased is through the penalty of sin being carried out. To say that Jesus appeased the wrath of God, then, is to say that Jesus received the wrath of God. God's wrath fell on him and burned itself out on him. There is, therefore, no wrath remaining for all those who will put their trust in what Jesus did on the cross.

It comes down to this: our sins will either be found on us or on Christ. If our sins are found on us, we will have to bear the penalty for them, which is eternal separation from God. If our sins are found on Christ, we will find that he has already bore their penalty.

Does this make sense to you? Are you trusting Christ? Are you trusting in his propitiation? Are you able to take as your own the following words of the hymn-writer, Augustus Toplady?

Nothing in my hand I bring,
Simply to Thy cross I cling.

In the words of our text, the apostle also raises another vital issue.

How can we know we are going to heaven?

John says: 'These things I have written to you who believe in the name of the Son of God, that you may know that you have eternal life, and that you may continue to believe in the name of the Son of God' (v. 13).

That verse immediately tells us that we have to look back to that which John has written in this epistle. Note, he says: 'These things I have written to you … that you may know that you have eternal life.'

So what has John said about this business of knowing that we have eternal life?

The confession test

The first is what we may refer to as the confession test. In this test he points his readers to the very same thing we noted in the words of Paul. In other words, he, John, points them to Christ as the ground of their hope.

'Do you want to know if you are truly saved?' he seems to ask. Then he answers in this way: 'What do you believe about Jesus Christ? Surely you know what you believe about him! If you can say Christ is the ground of your hope, all is well.'

Here it is in John's own words: 'Whoever confesses that Jesus is the Son of God, God abides in him, and he in God' (4:15).

But John does not leave it there. He seems to anticipate his readers asking this question: 'How do we know that we are truly trusting Christ as the ground of our hope?'

So he proceeds to give his readers two more tests.

The commandment test

John states this test in these words: 'Now by this we know that we know him, if we keep his commandments. He who says, "I know him," and does not keep his commandments, is a liar, and the truth is not in him' (2:3-4; see also 5:2-3).

No Christian perfectly keeps all the commandments of God. John's point is rather that the child of God takes the commandments of God very seriously. He affirms them as being good and right, he desires to keep them, he seeks to keep them and when he fails to do so he is troubled and miserable until he finally comes to repentance.

The love test

Then comes what we may refer to as the 'love' test. John puts it in these words: 'We know that we have passed from death to life, because we love the brethren. He who does not love his brother abides in death' (3:14; see also 2:9-11).

John's logic on this point is irrefutable. He says: 'If someone says, "I love God," and hates his brother, he is a liar; for he who does not love his brother whom he has seen, how can he love God whom he has not seen?' (4:20).

He was hearkening back, of course, to the words of the Lord Jesus on the night before he was crucified: 'By this all will know that you are my disciples, if you have love for one another' (John 13:35).

What does it mean to love our brothers and sisters in Christ? It certainly means to minister to them in time of need. It must surely include forgiving them when they offend us. It obviously means desiring to be with them in the house of God. (By the way, one of the best antidotes for doubt is regular worship in the house of God!)

These, then, are the three tests that John gives. How do we fare against them?

Looking to Christ

Before leaving this matter of assurance, I want to offer a word of caution about the tendency to look to our experience for assurance rather than looking to Christ.

Satan always tries to get us to look away from Christ as the ground of our hope. If he cannot keep us from going to heaven, he will at least try to make us go there without rejoicing along the way. Satan knows a doubting Christian is a miserable specimen. He is a poor recommendation of the Christian faith to unbelievers, and his doubt so consumes him that he is able to contribute very little to the work of Christ's kingdom.

So Satan is ever trying to shift the ground of our hope from Christ to something else. If we are not on our guard, he will shift it to our experience and will tell us it is impossible for us to be saved because we weren't emotional enough. Or he will shift it to our performance and assure us because our performance is less than it ought to be that we could not possibly be a Christian. There is no end to his devices.

But the wise Christian will not allow Satan to shift the ground of his hope. He will always point to the Lord Jesus Christ and his finished work on Calvary's cross and say to Satan: 'Find some fault in that, and then I will doubt!' How Satan flees when we take our refuge in the mighty Saviour and rub his nose in Calvary's love!

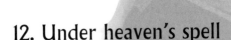

12. Under heaven's spell

Please read: 2 Corinthians 4:16-18; 2 Peter 3:11-14

The Lord calls us to be under heaven's spell. He calls us to be so intrigued by heaven and so fascinated with it that it makes a huge difference in how we live in the here and now. In other words, we are called to be heavenly-minded. Earth-dwellers with heavenly minds! That's what we are to be.

Sometimes people talk about the danger of being so heavenly-minded that we are of no earthly good. But the Bible tells us that the more heavenly-minded we are, the more good we shall do.

What is it to be heavenly-minded? It is thinking about heaven to the point that we can no longer think about things here in the same way. It is thinking about heaven to the point that our thinking about everything else is changed.

What are some things that are changed by thinking about heaven?

Our view of our problems and trials

Life brings many difficulties our way, and we find them very hard to bear and hard to understand. Why has God allowed this sickness? Why has this loved one died? Why is it so hard to make ends meet?

How does heaven help us with the hardships and heartaches of life? It first reminds us that these things are temporary. A better day is coming!

Television advertisements sometimes show people enjoying themselves in some way, and someone will say: 'It doesn't get any better than this!' For Christians, it does get better — a lot better! And our trials make us look forward to that better day when there will be no trials or tears.

The apostle Paul lived under heaven's spell. He was one heaven-intoxicated man. He thought about heaven in every circumstance, and his thinking made even the most difficult circumstances bearable. He writes: 'For I consider that the sufferings of this present time are not worthy to be compared with the glory which shall be revealed in us' (Romans 8:18).

He also says: 'For our light affliction, which is but for a moment, is working for us a far more exceeding and eternal weight of glory, while we do not look at the things which are seen, but at the things which are not seen. For the things which are seen are temporary, but the things which are not seen are eternal' (2 Corinthians 4:17-18).

David Charles puts it this way in his hymn:

And we, from the wilds of the desert,
Shall flee to the land of the blest;

Life's tears shall be changed to rejoicing,
Its labours and toils into rest:
There we shall find refuge eternal,
From sin, from affliction, from pain,
And in the sweet love of the Saviour,
A joy without end shall attain.

Our afflictions are temporary inconveniences on the road to eternal glory! Sam Storms observes: 'The strength to endure present suffering is the fruit of meditating on future satisfaction.'[1]

Our view of 'injustices'

Do you often find yourself wondering about life's inequities? As we look at our world, we see all kinds of suffering. Wars are raging. Mere children are being enslaved for the purposes of pornography and prostitution. Millions of children are being aborted, and many are being abused. We also have instances of the abuse of spouses and the elderly. And to all of these things, we can add the evils of murder and rape.

I have often wondered how loud the cry would be if we could take all the individual cries in this world and put them together. And the question that comes to mind is this: If we could package all these cries into one, would it be loud enough to reach heaven? In other words, does God care about all the heartaches, all the sufferings, all the inequities?

The Bible assures us that God is aware of them all, and he will eventually set everything right.

> There is a great day of adjustment coming! ... No evil will be left unpunished, and no righteousness will be unrewarded.

We may wonder all we want about the reasons God does not do more to correct inequities now, but we need not wonder about what he will do in the future. There is a great day of adjustment coming! All that seems now to be out of balance will then be brought into perfect balance. No evil will be left unpunished, and no righteousness will be unrewarded.

We need to be very clear on this: the same chapters of Revelation that describe heaven (chs 21 & 22) also tell us that many will not be there. Revelation 21:27 says: 'But there shall by no means enter it anything that defiles, or causes an abomination or a lie, but only those who are written in the Lamb's Book of Life.' And Revelation 22:15 adds: 'But outside are dogs and sorcerers and sexually immoral and murderers and idolaters, and whoever loves and practises a lie.'

Those who practise evil here will not be allowed to practise it there! And those of us who often lament evildoers getting off easy here will have nothing to lament there.

Ours is a time in which many get very angry when a pastor or anyone else has the audacity to talk about judgement and hell. I find this very interesting.

Do we really want God to let evildoers off? Do we want him to give a pass to those who marched through life harming others? Do we want God to let murderers, abusers and terrorists to walk free?

If we want our judges here to mete out justice and put criminals in penitentiaries, we should not object to God putting people in hell, which is his penitentiary!

If we expect the books to be balanced in this life, and every evil deed to be punished and every good to be rewarded, we are going to be sorely disappointed. Sam Storms is correct to say: 'If you insist on taking the short view of things you will be forever frustrated, confused, and angry.'[2]

Our view of death

The knowledge of heaven never impacts believers more than on the matter of death. Heaven takes the sting out of death.

The apostle Paul found it to be so. He writes: 'For to me, to live is Christ, and to die is gain' (Philippians 1:21). He also referred to death as departing to 'be with Christ'. And he considered that to be 'far better' (1:23). Paul's words led the great Charles Spurgeon to preach a sermon entitled 'The Saint's Deathday Better than His Birthday'.

How does the knowledge of heaven help us with death? It makes us realize that death is not the end. It makes us realize that death is a passageway or a doorway. Just as a door allows us to leave one room and go into another, so death allows us to leave this world and enter into heaven. The well-known author, Calvin Miller, expresses it in these words:

I once scorned ev'ry fearful thought of death,
When it was but the end of pulse and breath,
But now my eyes have seen that past the pain

There is a world waiting to be claimed.
Earthmaker, Holy, let me now depart,
For living's such a temporary art.
And dying is but getting dressed for God,
Our graves are merely doorways cut in sod.[3]

Five months before he died, C. S. Lewis wrote to a woman who feared that her own death was imminent. Lewis said, 'Can you not see death as a friend and deliverer? ... What is there to be afraid of? ... Your sins are confessed... Has this world been so kind to you that you should leave with regret? There are better things ahead than we leave behind... Our Lord says to you, "Peace, child, peace. Relax. Let go. I will catch you. Do you trust me so little?" ... Of course, this may not be the end. Then make it a good rehearsal.'

Lewis signed the letter, 'Yours (and like you, a tired traveller, near the journey's end)'.[4]

Heaven, then, yields wonderful benefits before we ever get there! It transforms our thinking about life's afflictions, life's injustices and life's end. But heaven does not do this apart from some effort on our part. We must think about heaven! The apostle Peter urged his readers to fully 'set' their hope 'on the grace' that would be brought to them 'at the revelation of Jesus Christ' (1 Peter 1:13, ESV).

Regarding this matter of setting the hope, Sam Storms writes: 'This is a commanded obsession. Fixate fully! Rivet your soul on the grace that you will receive when Christ returns. Tolerate no distractions. Entertain no diversions. Don't let your mind be swayed. Devote every ounce of mental and spiritual and emotional energy to concentrating and contemplating on the grace that is to come.'[5]

13. Treasure in heaven

Please read: Matthew 6:19-21

These verses present us with one of the most exciting prospects imaginable. We can accumulate treasure in heaven! We have this from no less an authority than the Lord Jesus Christ. He commands his disciples to 'lay up' for themselves 'treasures in heaven'.

What does this mean? What is it to 'lay up' treasure in heaven? Believers in Christ have understood this teaching in different ways.

Doing things that have everlasting effects

This is how John R. W. Stott understands it: '...we may say that to "lay up treasure in heaven" is to do anything on earth whose effects last for eternity.'[1]

What are some things we can do now that will have everlasting effects?

Using our money

The first and most obvious answer has to do with the use of our material resources. This is what Jesus had on his mind when he spoke these words.

Craig L. Blomberg writes:

> Spiritual treasure should be defined as broadly as possible — as everything that believers can take with them beyond the grave — e.g. holiness of character, obedience to all of God's commandments, souls won for Christ, and disciples nurtured in the faith. In this context, however, storing up treasures focuses particularly on the compassionate use of material resources to meet others' physical and spiritual needs, in keeping with priorities of God's kingdom...[2]

Ever the keen reader of men, Jesus could tell that many of his listeners were in the grip of concern for amassing as much material wealth as they could.

Now the Bible never tells us that it is wrong for us to have material possessions. No one has stated it better than Warren Wiersbe: 'It is not wrong for us to possess things, but it is wrong for things to possess us.'[3]

Jesus was calling his hearers to not be possessed by their possessions. And he gave very good and sound reasons. The first is that material wealth is notoriously uncertain and unpredictable. Moth and rust corrupt and thieves break in and steal! (v. 19).

The second reason Jesus gave is that there is a higher good to be achieved with our wealth than merely accumulating it. That higher good is using it. His teaching is that we can actually use our wealth in such a way as to achieve eternal good!

Think about it! We can use our wealth on things that will soon perish. In other words, we can use our wealth to buy things that will not last. Or we can use it to win souls for Christ and to advance the kingdom of God. Which makes more sense — buying another trinket that will soon perish, or doing something of eternal value?

Sam Storms writes:

> 'It is not wrong for us to possess things, but it is wrong for things to possess us.'

> If there awaits us an eternal inheritance of immeasurable glory, it is senseless to expend effort and energy here, sacrificing so much time and money, to obtain for so brief a time in corruptible form what we will enjoy forever in consummate perfection.[4]

Praying

Another thing of eternal value that we can do is to pray. I wonder how many of us realize this! The Bible teaches that God preserves the prayers of his people, which is another way of saying that our prayers are never lost!

When we finally get home to heaven, we will find our prayers there waiting for us. The apostle John writes: 'Now when he had taken the scroll, the four living creatures and the twenty-four elders fell down before the Lamb, each having a harp, and golden bowls full of incense, which are the prayers of the saints' (Revelation 5:8; see also 8:3-4). When we pray, we do something of everlasting value!

Reaching others

A third such way is to use whatever means we have at our disposal to reach others for Christ. We have already mentioned the use of our money to this end, but there are other things we can do as well. Daniel 12:3 says:

> Those who are wise shall shine
> Like the brightness of the firmament,
> And those who turn many to righteousness
> Like the stars forever and ever.

The truth of the matter is that we are each living in a vast field which offers us multitudes of souls for spiritual harvest. Jesus made this point to his disciples: 'Behold, I say to you, lift up your eyes and look at the fields, for they are already white for harvest! And he who reaps receives wages, and gathers fruit for eternal life, that both he who sows and he who reaps may rejoice together' (John 4:35b-36).

One of the things that will make heaven more heavenly is to find there individuals who were saved because the Lord was pleased to use our attempts to spread the gospel.

Doing things that will receive a reward

The things we have already noticed will be rewards. To enter heaven and find those who have been saved through our influence and to find our own prayers there will be to us wonderful rewards indeed. But will there be other rewards in addition to those?

Tremendous debate swirls around this issue! And many adamantly deny any such rewards, believing that the concept brings into our Christian service an ulterior motive. We are to serve because we love the Lord Jesus, not out of the expectation for a reward. Such is their argument.

No one can object to the contention that we are to serve because we love the Lord. But the other side of the argument is that God has, out of the goodness and kindness of his heart, very definitely promised rewards to those who serve him faithfully. It is certainly not wrong to anticipate that which God himself has promised!

Sometimes the Bible refers to rewards in terms of wages (Matthew 5:12; 6:4,6,18; 10:40-42). It also speaks of rewards in terms of a crown (1 Corinthians 9:25; Philippians 4:1; 1 Thessalonians 2:19; 2 Timothy 4:8; James 1:12; 1 Peter 5:4; Revelation 3:11). And it sometimes depicts rewards as a matter of standing or rank, that is, as a matter of being greatest or least in heaven (Matthew 18:1-4; 20:20-28; Luke 22:24-30).[5]

Many find the suggestion that some will be greater in heaven than others to be especially distasteful. They cherish the notion that we all will be exactly alike in every way.

To the question of whether we will all be alike in heaven, William Hendriksen answers: '...Yes, in the sense that all who enter there will have been sinners who are then in the state of having been "saved by grace". All, moreover, will owe their salvation equally to the sovereign love of God. And the goal for all will be the same: to glorify God and enjoy him for ever. Nevertheless, there will be inequalities, differences, degrees of weal (and in hell degrees of woe).'[6]

Paul Helm states: 'There will be differences in heaven. The heavenly citizens are not clones, nor the product of a celestial assembly-line. They are individuals who retain their individuality. And some will enjoy a different status in heaven from others.'[7]

We have seen, then, that we are right to expect rewards because God has promised them. But we can and must go further. The same God who has promised rewards commands us to earnestly seek them.

The apostle Paul writes: 'Do you not know that those who run in a race all run, but one receives the prize? Run in such a way that you may obtain it. And everyone who competes for the prize is temperate in all things. Now they do it to obtain a perishable crown, but we for an imperishable crown. Therefore, I run thus: not with uncertainty. Thus I fight: not as one who beats the air. But I discipline my body and bring it into subjection, lest, when I have preached to others, I myself should become disqualified' (1 Corinthians 9:24-27).

The apostle John adds: 'Look to yourselves, that we do not lose those

> The same God who has promised rewards commands us to earnestly seek them.

things we worked for, but that we may receive a full reward' (2 John 8). Jonathan Edwards, no average Bible scholar, does not hesitate to say: 'We ought to seek high degrees of glory in heaven.'[8] It would be one thing if we were desiring great rewards in heaven when we had no command to do so; it is quite another to desire them because we have been so commanded.

The piercing question before each of us is this: are we going about our work here with heaven and heaven's rewards in view? To put it in the words of our Lord: 'Are we laying up treasure for ourselves in heaven?'

I can well imagine us coming home to heaven with regret that we have not done more to lay up treasure there. It is hard to imagine us coming there with regret that we have laid up so much treasure there. Let us, then, be working with heaven in view.

14. Home before dark

Please read: Isaiah 60:19-20; Revelation 21:23,25; 22:5

Vance Havner, a well-known American evangelist, recalls a rule that his father had for him when he was a boy, namely, that he was always to be home before dark.

When he was a teenager, he went into the gospel ministry. Often in those days he would go to his preaching assignments by train. He relates with fondness seeing his father waiting when his train pulled into the station.

Drawing on those memories, Havner shared the first words that he was planning to say to his father upon meeting him in glory: 'You remember back in the country when I was a little boy, no matter where I was in the afternoon I was supposed to be back by sundown. It's been a long trip, Dad, but here I am by the grace of God, home before dark.'[1]

That phrase 'home before dark' set me thinking. Heaven is home for believers in Christ, and all of them will finally make it there. And when they get there, they will be able to say that they 'got home before dark'.

Eternal darkness

We are living in days in which most people dismiss any talk of eternal judgement. It has all been decided. An opinion poll was taken. Most people found the thought to be unpleasant. So there must be no such thing as eternal judgement!

But to dismiss the concept of hell is to dismiss the teaching of the Bible, and, more particularly, the teaching of the Lord Jesus Christ. The Bible describes hell in various ways, and one of the most sobering is that it is a place of darkness. The apostle Peter speaks of 'the blackness of darkness' being 'reserved for ever' for unbelievers (2 Peter 2:17).

And Jude mentions 'the blackness of darkness' being 'reserved' for the ungodly (Jude 13). There is, then, such a thing as eternal darkness.

With this as our backdrop, we can proceed to say something that is wonderful indeed.

No darkness in heaven

The apostle John makes this very clear in his description of his vision of the New Jerusalem: 'The city had no need of the sun or of the moon to shine in it, for the glory of God illuminated it. The Lamb is its light' (Revelation 21:23). A bit later he adds: 'there shall be no night there' (21:25). Still later, he says, 'There shall be no night there: They need no lamp nor light of the sun, for the Lord God gives them light. And they shall reign for ever and ever' (22:5).

To come home to heaven, then, is to come to the place of light. It is to miss out on the darkness. All of God's people will be able to say that they made it home before dark!

We cannot leave this thought of God's people getting home before dark without reminding ourselves of one very crucial thing.

> To come home to heaven, then, is to come to the place of light.

Jesus in darkness

The people of God will not experience eternal darkness because Jesus experienced it for them on the cross.

Do you recall that when the Lord Jesus was crucified, the land was enveloped in deep darkness for three hours? There has never been such darkness. The darkness of the darkest night could not equal it. It was so dark that one could not see his hand in front of his face. It was, in the words of William Hendriksen, 'intense and unforgettable'.

What an incredible thing! Jesus was the one who dispelled the darkness! There was that pathetic man who was possessed with a legion of demons. Living among the tombs, he went about shrieking in anguish and terrorizing the people who tried time after time to bind him without success. The darkness of sin and despair was written all over him, but Jesus set him free (Mark 5:1-20).

Then there was Jairus, the man whose daughter died while he was trying to get Jesus to come and heal her. Jairus' servants sadly said, 'Your daughter is dead. Why trouble the Teacher any further?' (Mark 5:35). But death was no trouble for Jesus. He went with Jairus, took the little girl by the hand and drove the darkness of death away (Mark 5:41-42).

A man, blind from birth, seemed to be a hopeless case. But Jesus, the darkness-dispeller, anointed his eyes and sent him to wash in the pool of Siloam. The man soon returned, saying, '…I went and washed, and I received sight' (John 9:11). It is no wonder that Jesus said, 'As long as I am in the world, I am the light of the world' (John 9:5). Light followed Jesus wherever he went, and darkness fled before him.

But on the cross he was shrouded in deepest darkness. Why? The answer lies in the nature of what Jesus was doing on that cross. He was there as the sin-bearer for his people. He did not have any sins of his own, but he went to that cross to receive the penalty of God against the sins of his people.

Jesus was on the cross to experience hell itself so his people will never have to experience it. Jesus himself explained the darkness when he cried: 'My God, my God, why have you forsaken me?' (Matthew 27:46).

Hell is the place of separation from God and, as such, it is the place of ultimate darkness. If Jesus was there to endure hell, it was essential for him to be enveloped in darkness.

William Hendriksen was certainly correct in saying, 'Hell came to Calvary that day, and the Saviour descended into it and bore its horrors in our stead.'[2]

It comes down to one fundamental proposition: Jesus refused to dispel the darkness of Calvary so that he could dispel the darkness of sinners.

Those who enter heaven will do so because Jesus entered their darkness! And when they enter, the prophecy of Zechariah will be gloriously fulfilled:

> …at evening time it shall happen
> That it will be light
>
> (Zechariah 14:7).

The evening of life in this world will not be followed by the night of darkness but rather by the dawning of eternal life.

Let's go back to Reepicheep. At one point in the voyage, he speaks of his quest for Aslan's land: 'While I can, I sail in the Dawn Treader. When she fails me, I paddle east in my coracle. When she sinks, I shall swim east with my four paws. And when I can swim no longer, if I have not reached Aslan's country … I shall sink with my nose to the sunrise…'[3]

While Reepicheep's yearning for Aslan's land may encourage us to yearn for Immanuel's land, we do not have to worry about sinking with our noses to the sunrise. All who trust in Jesus Christ will most certainly enter into heaven's glory — home before dark! Before hell reaches its full and final form, God's

The evening of life in this world will not be followed by the night of darkness but rather by the dawning of eternal life.

119

people will already be safe in heaven. And there they will join together in these majestic and happy words:

> Worthy is the Lamb who was slain
> To receive power and riches and wisdom,
> And strength and honour and glory and blessing!
> (Revelation 5:12).

Notes

Introduction

1. Cited by Randy Alcorn, *Heaven*, Tyndale House Publishers Inc., p.445.
2. John Bunyan, *The Pilgrim's Progress*, Zondervan Publishing House, p.17.

Chapter 1 — The one who has the right…

1. Alexander Maclaren, *Expositions of Holy Scripture: John 1-10*, Baker Book House, vol. x, pp.269-70.
2. Matthew Henry, *Matthew Henry's Commentary*, Fleming H. Revell Company, vol. v, p.885.
3. W. A. Criswell & Paige Patterson, *Heaven*, Tyndale House Publishers Inc., p.16.

Chapter 2 — Why should we be interested…?

1. No author given, *Four Great Certainties*, Present Truth, p.7.
2. Charles Spurgeon, *The Treasury of David*, vol. i, p.371.

Chapter 3 — Heaven is a present reality

1. William Hendriksen, *The Bible on the Life Hereafter*, Baker Book House, p.39.
2. Geoffrey B. Wilson, *2 Corinthians*, The Banner of Truth Trust, pp.65-6.

Chapter 4 — Crossing the swelling tide

1. A similar chapter appears in my book, *A Promise is a Promise*, Evangelical Press, pp.175-9.
2. Bunyan, *The Pilgrim's Progress*, p.144.
3. As above, pp.145-6.

Chapter 8 — The heaven of heaven

1. Don Fortner, *Discovering Christ in Revelation*, Evangelical Press, p.453.
2. Alcorn, *Heaven*, p.166.
3. Bunyan, *The Pilgrim's Progress*, p.286.
4. Charles Spurgeon, *Metropolitan Tabernacle Pulpit*, Pilgrim Publications, vol. xxiii, p.343.
5. As above, pp.343-4.

Chapter 9 — The Father's house

1. J. C. Ryle, *Expository Thoughts on John*, The Banner of Truth Trust, vol. iii, p.55.

Chapter 10 — Jewels gathered

1. Alan Redpath, *Faith for the Times*, vol. ii, p.17.
2. T. V. Moore, *Zechariah, Haggai & Malachi*, The Banner of Truth Trust, pp.167-8.

Chapter 12 — Under heaven's spell

1. Sam Storms, *One Thing*, Christian Focus, p.167.
2. As above, p.166.
3. Alcorn, *Heaven*, p.447.
4. As above.
5. Storms, p.165.

Chapter 13 — Treasure in heaven

1. John R. W. Stott, *The Message of the Sermon on the Mount*, Inter-Varsity Press, p.156.
2. Craig L. Blomberg, *New American Commentary: Matthew*, Broadman Press, p.23.
3. Warren Wiersbe, *The Bible Exposition Commentary*, Victor Books, vol. i, p.27.
4. Storms, *One Thing*, p.164.
5. I am indebted to Eryl Davies, *Heaven is a Far Better Place*, for his discussion of rewards and for his summation of biblical passages, pp.213-33. The book is published by Evangelical Press.
6. Hendriksen, *The Bible on the Life Hereafter*, pp.93-4.
7. Cited by Davies, *Heaven is a Far Better Place*, p.214.
8. As above.

Chapter 14 — Home before dark

1. Vance Havner, *On This Rock I Stand*, Baker Book House, pp.151-2.
2. William Hendriksen, *New Testament Commentary: Luke*, Baker Book House, p.1034.
3. Alcorn, *Heaven*, p.445.

What the Bible

teaches about

angels

ANGELS in movies, television shows, figurines, books, magazine articles and seminars — angels are everywhere!

This would seem to be very good news. After all, the Bible does have a lot to say about angels, mentioning them 273 times. Should we not welcome such widespread interest in a biblical topic?

Yet interest in a biblical topic is of no value if we are not biblical about the topic. All too often, the only connection between the current angel-mania and the Bible is the teaching that angels exist.

In this straightforward and easy-to-read book in the *What the Bible teaches about…* series Roger Ellsworth sets the record straight, putting the biblical view of angels in a clear and helpful way, dealing with such topics as what are the seraphim and cherubim, angels as ministering spirits, and the role of angels at the beginning and end of time. Above all, however, is his concern to drive us to the one the angels themselves adore — the Lord Jesus Christ.

Roger Ellsworth, Evangelical Press, 128 pages,
ISBN-13 978-0-85234-617-4; ISBN 0-85234-617-4

What the Bible

teaches about

worship

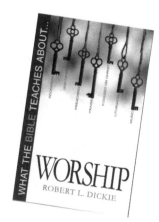

It is the author's belief that there is in these days a stirring within the Church of Jesus Christ. People are hungering and thirsting for a deeper and richer experience of the presence of God in worship. Many of the Lord's people are growing tired with the superficial and silly innovations that have been substituted for the worship of God, and which have been the cause of so many debates, struggles and conflicts within the church.

What is worship? How do we worship? What is acceptable worship?

In this thoroughly biblical and immensely practical work Pastor Bob Dickie answers such questions by directing us to the clearest example of worship in the Scriptures. In Revelation chapters 4 and 5 the Lord pulls back the curtains and allows us to get a glimpse of what true, biblical worship is. It should be centred on Christ and reflect the example of worship that is taking place in the throne-room of heaven right now.

Robert L. Dickie, Evangelical Press, 160 pages,
ISBN-13   978-0-85234-659-4   ISBN 0-85234-659-X

A wide range of Christian books is available from Evangelical Press. If you would like a free catalogue please write to us or contact us by e-mail. Alternatively, you can view the whole catalogue online at our web site:

www.evangelicalpress.org.

Evangelical Press
Faverdale North, Darlington, DL3 0PH, England

e-mail: sales@evangelicalpress.org

Evangelical Press USA
P. O. Box 825, Webster, New York 14580, USA

e-mail: usa.sales@evangelicalpress.org